seasonal home cooking

seasonal home cooking

simple food with fresh ingredients

Bridget Jones

APPLE

CONTENTS

SUCCESS WITH SEASONAL COOKING

In an age where global choice is heralded as the best thing to happen to food, it's easy to forget that the freshest, tastiest produce is usually grown close to home. By allowing our dietary habits to be influenced by the seasons, we can enjoy healthy, flavoursome fare that often seems just right for the weather. Benefits extend beyond the palate, too – just a little knowledge about how to choose, prepare and preserve nature's finest ingredients makes seasonal cooking an easy, inexpensive option for today's cook.

Shopping for seasonal best

Making the most of seasonal produce is all about selective shopping – checking out the source of supply and picking through produce to find succulent roots, shoots and leaves that are bursting with goodness. Reading labels may not be the most romantic of selection methods but it is a first step to making the right choice. As well as the country of origin, the location of the grower is often included – you may well have the choice of purchasing produce that was harvested just a few miles away.

FARM SHOPS

Fields of green vegetables or orchards full of ripening fruit are sure signs that good local produce will soon be available, if it is not already on display. Major supermarket chains are extremely picky about the look of fruit and vegetables, accepting only model items of even size and form. This means that the slightly small, misshapen or irregular produce is often available in farm shops. While the "look" may be less than designer, the quality and flavour are usually excellent, and buying from the grower often ensures the food is fresh. It is also still possible to purchase at the farm gate in some areas – look out for signs indicating that seasonal crops are for sale.

SPECIALIST SUPPLIERS

Practical alternatives to supermarkets include specialist suppliers, such as fishmongers, butchers and delicatessens. Mail order and e-commerce along with fruit and vegetable box-schemes are popular means of trading. The quality is usually excellent and established companies ensure customers receive reliable deliveries.

MARKETS

Weekly markets are great places to find quality at a good price. Whereas supermarkets prefer produce that is under-ripe and immature to allow for handling and long display, market traders usually offer fruit and vegetables that are ready for eating. The price is competitive and the quality is good, even if it does not have as long a shelf life. Local butchers, egg producers, fishmongers and cheese makers often have stalls at town markets, and this is a great place to quiz farmers or their representatives about the way in which animals are reared, crops grown or food products manufactured.

RICH PICKINGS

Garden produce, wild foods and pick-your-own outlets are the ultimate choices for freshness and economy. A vegetable patch is a source of relaxation as well as fabulous food and with the right planning it does not have to be overdemanding. Focusing on crops that thrive with the minimum of attention is perfectly possible – a local nursery or garden centre is the best source of advice. Even a small garden or patio can provide worthwhile rewards for very little effort.. Vegetables, such as sprouting broccoli, beans and peas, can be grown in flower borders. Herbs bring a brilliant seasonal twist to dishes that may well be served throughout the year; grow them in flower beds or window boxes, hanging baskets or tubs, if a herb garden is not an option.

Equipment for the seasonal kitchen

The seasons influence how we choose to cook as much as the ingredients we buy. A seasonal *batterie de cuisine*, or set of cooking equipment, enables the more adventurous cook to conjure up all kinds of seasonal treats with the minimum amount of fuss.

POTS AND PANS

This is one area of cooking for which a few specialist items are particularly useful, and in some cases essential.

- A preserving pan is large and wide, designed to allow maximum evaporation when boiling jams and similar preserves. A sugar thermometer is useful when testing for setting point.

- Straining equipment is essential for making jellies. A muslin (cheesecloth) bag should be thoroughly washed, boiled and dried before being packed in a plastic bag for storage when not in use. A stand for holding the bag is optional but far more practical than rigging it up over an upturned stool. The stand should be thoroughly washed and dried before being folded away and stored.

- It is well worth buying two dozen or so preserving pots with replacement lids. As they are emptied, the containers should be washed, sterilized and thoroughly dried before storage. Check lids or sealing devices before using them next time and replace if necessary.

- An asparagus steamer is invaluable if you plan to eat a lot of this delicious vegetable. It consists of a tall, narrow pan with a metal basket inside. The basket holds a bundle of asparagus with the stalks in the boiling water, while at the same time supporting the tender tips upright so that they can cook in the steam.

- A fish kettle is a long, thin and deep pan containing a rack for cooking fish whole. It is a favourite of those who like to poach wild salmon in the spring.

- Shallow, multi-layered steamers are perfect for cooking little mounds of tender spring and summer vegetables. The deep and wide type can fit big bowls filled with hearty winter puddings.

- Big stockpots are put to most use during winter months, when soups are in demand. Casseroles, stew pots and slow cookers are in the same category – most valuable in winter, but so useful that they will rarely be confined to the back of the cupboard during warmer months.

- Pans that are decommissioned for the season should be thoroughly washed, dried and cleaned according to material type. A suitable metal cleaner or polish should be used so that the pans are gleaming like new before they are stored.

STORING BARBECUE EQUIPMENT

It is worth taking time to store barbecue equipment safely, to prevent rusting in damp weather. Too often unused barbecues are left out in the garden during rainy weather.

- All cooking racks should be dismantled, brushed clean and scrubbed, then dried and covered before storing in a dry place.

- Gas canisters should be disconnected and stored according to the manufacturer's instructions. Barbecue fuel does not keep well, so it should be used up before the end of the season; however, any leftovers can be stored in a closed waterproof bag.

- Similarly, all the cooking utensils should be thoroughly washed or scrubbed and dried. Damaged or rusty items should be discarded.

SPACE-SAVING STORAGE

When cupboard space is limited, lidded plastic boxes are ideal for storing utensils, serving dishes and glassware that is likely to be out of use for some time. Soft white kitchen paper or plastic bubble wrap can be interleaved with fragile items rather than dirty printed newspaper. High cupboards may not be the ideal storage place for everyday items but they are fine for equipment that is rarely used. The garage, or a garden shed, are suitable for storing items packed in tightly covered plastic boxes.

Spring
Cooking

INTRODUCTION

Spring is a wonderfully positive season. Lengthening days and brighter weather bring a sense of energy that influences appetite as well as activity. Young produce is just becoming available from local suppliers and many garden owners have rows of tiny vegetables ready for thinning out and sampling. Pots of herbs on a sheltered patio produce an abundance of new shoots to bring fresh and lively flavours to simple cooking. There are several good reasons for bothering to find seasonal specialities: from a purely culinary angle, the fresher the food, the better its condition and flavour, and the easier it is to cook; fresh food is more nutritious, because the vitamin value diminishes with staleness; and last, but by no means least, buying food in season can be economical.

Special in spring

Sunlight, warmth and spring rain encourage rapid growth, and it is difficult to resist the temptation to pick too many seedlings or young shoots from a vegetable plot or herb tub. While the average garden offers a small yield, commercial growers have brought on their produce to fill the shelves and markets with crisp young vegetables.

BABY VEGETABLES

Look for little leeks, spring onions (scallions) and spring greens (collards): these deliciously tender young leaves grow from cut cabbage stumps to provide oodles of versatile flavour for little cost. Tall purple sprouting broccoli is absolutely bursting with flavour, but its season is short, so catch it while you can. The first leaves of Swiss chard, young spinach and sorrel go well together or separately in salads or cooked dishes.

Baby carrots are irresistibly sweet and their tender tops are deliciously fresh in salads or used herb-style in cooked dishes. Young broad (fava) beans come into the

shops and the small pods are a particular treat. Globe artichokes also feature; look for young Italian vegetables in which the chokes have not yet formed, and cook them whole. Young peas and tender mangetouts (snow peas) are full of flavour.

Young vine leaves are readily available outdoors in some regions or from a greenhouse vine in cooler areas. A short spell of hot weather brings up the asparagus shoots and it is time to indulge at the first signs because the season is short.

Fresh mint and chives sprout up to become the favourite spring herbs but there is also new growth on established plants, such as bay, rosemary and sage.

TENDER MEAT AND FISH

Spring lamb is the seasonal star – tender, sweet cutlets (rib chops) are perfect for grilling (broiling) while racks and legs make succulent and aromatic roasts. Traditionally, spring is also the time for chicken, especially young spring chicken or poussin. Guinea fowl is a good choice for a lighter style of casserole: it is at its prime at this time of year.

The availability of local fish and seafood depends on the weather, but there is always a good choice of white or firm fish from around the world. Select flat fish, such as sole, plaice or flounder and make the most of shellfish for delicate flavour and texture, opting for firm tuna for main dishes that are satisfying without being over-rich.

REFRESHING SWEETS

Rhubarb is the vegetable that is treated as a fruit in culinary terms. Forced rhubarb is available in early spring, followed by the main crop which will be past its edible best by summer. The tart, fruity stalks make tempting puddings and refreshing desserts. There are still juicy seedless oranges and zesty thin-skinned lemons to add a citrus lift to savoury and sweet cooking, giving recipes a light spring feel.

Culinary combinations

By tradition, spring is the season for fresh and lively combinations – bitter balanced by sweet, rich resolved by sharp. Success is found in speed and simplicity, a move away from the complex, long-cooked dishes of winter, taking care not to drown the first precious fresh produce and using the new herbs to enliven year-round foods. Try some of these flavours together with lighter styles of cooking like stir-frying and steaming.

- Use the first small vine leaves to cover the breast meat of poussin before roasting and serving with a salad of hot new potatoes with grapes and roast garlic cloves.

- Mint is the perfect foil for rich duck – use it in combination with lemon, lime or orange to enliven the pan juices from roasting or grilling (broiling) breast fillets. Add a little honey and cider vinegar for a sweet–sour balance.

- Give grilled or pan-fried pork a spring lift by sprinkling with chopped fresh mint and grated lime rind just before serving. Deglaze the pan juices with a little lime juice and a good pinch of sugar.

- Combine finely shredded spring greens (collards) and chard with chopped spring onions (scallions) and mint in a lively stir-fry vegetable base for serving pan-fried pork fillet.

- Make the most of baby new potatoes by serving them as the focus for a main-course salad. Toss the freshly cooked potatoes in a little olive oil, grated lemon rind and chopped chives, and then serve on a bed of baby spinach and garnish with chopped hard-boiled egg.

- Complement tender steamed broad (fava) beans with diced lean cooked ham and lots of chopped parsley for a first course or light lunch.

- Serve freshly cooked asparagus tips with creamy scrambled eggs and thin slices of crisp wholemeal (whole-wheat) toast for a superlative spring brunch.

- Blanch new potatoes until barely tender, and then skewer them with strips of prosciutto and brush with olive oil before grilling until golden.

- When purple sprouting broccoli is fresh and tender, serve the lightly boiled spears on a plain risotto flavoured with a little lemon and chives, and dress with melted butter.

- Rhubarb is delicious with lamb or duck: make a simple sauce of sliced rhubarb cooked with sugar until tender, then enrich it with a little port. Serve warm or cool as a condiment to accompany roast lamb or duck.

- Select firm fish fillets or steaks for grilling, season lightly and serve topped with pats of simple lemon and chive butter. Add new potatoes and little mangetout (snow peas) or lightly steamed spinach.

- Warm salads are just right for spring and make a meal in themselves. Quickly pan-fry scallops in a little olive oil, toss gently and season well, and then pile on a large salad of shredded young spinach, tender young parsley sprigs, small whole mint leaves and chopped spring onions. Complement the flavours by adding some segments of orange, drizzle with a good salad dressing and serve immediately.

A fresh approach

While hearty meals are still welcome on cool days, there is a universal urge to eat lighter dishes. Spring is a good time to ease gradually into a natural change of eating patterns.

VIBRANT SOUPS

Hot soup is still welcome, especially when it is enlivened with tender young vegetables in a light broth. Aim for a result that is finely cut and refreshing rather than overfilling. Garnish with finely shredded pancakes and chopped fresh herbs. When the weather is warmer, introduce cool soups that make the most of spring leaves and herbs in cooking.

STEAMING SPECIALITIES

Steaming is especially useful for lightening flavours and creating clean textures. Steam fish, vegetables or poultry wrapped in foil for maximum flavour retention. Include bay leaves, chives, parsley and the young fronds of fennel to taste. Strips of lemon, lime or orange rind, chopped spring onions (scallions) and fresh root ginger are lively additions.

LIGHT CASSEROLES

Select tender cuts – seafood, poultry or meat suitable for pan-frying – instead of tougher pieces that require hours in the oven. Sauté spring onions with a little celery and carrot before pan-frying the main ingredients. Use cider, white wine and chicken stock for light sauces and add baby vegetables towards the end of cooking so that they are still slightly crisp in the cooked casserole. Finally, instead of thickening the juices, use a slotted spoon to transfer the ingredients to a serving dish and reduce the cooking liquor to intensify its flavour by boiling rapidly in the open pan. Enrich it with a little cream, if you like, before pouring over the casserole ingredients.

SPEEDY STIR-FRIES

Lamb fillet, chicken breast and duck breast are ideal for stir-frying with aromatics and/or finely cut, tender vegetables. Balancing modest portions of meat with generous amounts of vegetables lightens meals. Instead of finishing stir-fries with thickened sauces, lace them with aromatic oil flavoured with garlic or chilli and wedges of lemon. Alternatively, try serving lightly stir-fried meat or fish on a bed of lettuce as a warm salad.

SUCCULENT GRILLS AND ROASTS

Marinate chops, fillets and steaks with olive oil, garlic, and orange rind and juice or a little balsamic vinegar before grilling (broiling). Complement with simple condiments of chopped herbs in plain yogurt – try finely shredded sorrel or chopped chives and mint.

Roast young lamb on a bed of rosemary and whole garlic cloves for fabulous flavour. Bring spring zest to roast chicken by lining the base of the roasting tin with sliced lemons and bay leaves and serve with fresh new potatoes.

Keep it simple

Young, new produce requires the minimum of attention, which means less kitchen time for more goodness on the plate. The following are essential techniques and basic cooking suggestions for a few spring specialities.

ASPARAGUS

Succulent young asparagus needs no more than washing. If the spears are long, snap or cut off any tough or woody ends, feeling along to where they break off easily. Cook young spears in a frying pan of simmering water for 5–7 minutes.

- Blanch young spears for 3 minutes, drain and brown in a little olive oil on a very hot griddle. Serve with lemon.
- Tie larger spears that need longer cooking in bundles and simmer in boiling water in a tall asparagus kettle or deep pan, keeping the tips out of the water (tent foil over the top of a pan if the asparagus stands above the rim). Allow 10–20 minutes.

SORREL

Tender, long sorrel leaves are similar in appearance to spinach. Their flavour is tangy and lemony. Sorrel is used to flavour sauces and stuffings, but the small young leaves are also good finely shredded in salads and make a delicious soup.

- Mix shredded sorrel into a salad of baby spinach and spring onions (scallions).
- Toss shredded sorrel into stir-fried finely sliced leeks.

BROAD/FAVA BEANS

Very young broad bean pods can be cooked whole. As the pods mature, the versatile beans inside can be cooked in many ways.

- Trim the ends off baby pods of broad beans and cook them whole in boiling water for 5 minutes, then serve with butter or olive oil.

- Cook shelled beans in boiling water for about 5 minutes. Blanch beans in boiling water for 2–3 minutes, or until just tender, then drain, rinse in cold water and remove the pale skins. Toss the bright green beans in a little butter or olive oil.

- Crumbled, crisp-grilled (broiled) prosciutto or crisp-fried pancetta is delicious with broad beans. Thyme, tarragon and summer savory are complementary herbs.

GLOBE ARTICHOKES

Whole baby young globe artichoke buds are edible before the choke forms. Trim off the stalk, any tough outer leaves and the tough tip, and then cut into quarters. Cook in boiling water for 5–10 minutes, or until tender. Alternatively, fry in butter or olive oil.

- To prepare a mature artichoke, slice off the top and discard the large, open outer leaves around the base. Snip off the points, then use a small sharp knife to remove the choke and surrounding yellow leaves from the middle. Drop into water, acidulated with a few drops of lemon or vinegar. Boil for 15–20 minutes, or until tender.

- When serving cold, remove the artichoke's outer leaves once cooked. Trim off the top and points, then ease back the leaves and pull out the yellow leaves and choke, easing it off the tender cooked base (heart) with a teaspoon.

SPRING ONIONS/SCALLIONS

Trim off the roots and tips of spring onions, then pan-fry them whole for about 1 minute in olive oil with lots of sliced garlic. Serve topped with lemon rind and chopped parsley or use as a topping for a dish of hot, boiled potatoes.

RHUBARB

Young slim rhubarb stalks are tender, and if sliced into short lengths they cook quickly in a little water with sugar – about 5 minutes' poaching is enough. Older stalks may be stringy and any tough strings should be peeled off. Allow 10 minutes to cook the larger pieces, being careful not to overcook into a pulp.

- Fresh root or dried powdered ginger complements rhubarb – add when cooking. Try adding orange rind in the pan when cooking.

- Use rhubarb in sweet pies, crumbles and baked puddings; cold rhubarb purée makes excellent creams, such as fruit fool.

- Rhubarb is excellent for chutneys and savoury sauces, especially in sweet–sour combinations.

Cleanse and revitalize

Lighter appetites and cooking styles make spring an ideal time to detoxify through diet, and give the body a shake-up with suitable exercise. Livened up by the first fresh local produce of the year, a spring diet generates an immediate sense of wellbeing in preparation for summer.

GETTING STARTED

The general approach to detoxifying is to eat lighter, with less meat and poultry, more fruit and vegetables, and plenty of cleansing drinks. Reduce caffeine-rich tea and coffee intake, and avoid alcohol if you can. Cut down on refined carbohydrates, such as white bread, pasta and rice, and especially sugar – in all its forms. Lighten up on fat and calories by opting for yogurt instead of cream. It's also best to avoid processed foods, and eat lots of raw and lightly-cooked vegetables.

REVIVING DRINKS

Herbal or fruit teas are excellent alternatives to coffee and tea at the start of a cleansing diet routine. Fresh rosemary, the first sprigs of mint, and peppery sage make fabulous cleansing drinks. Instead of traditional herb teas, try a few herb sprigs steeped in boiling water with a combination of apple juice and lemon or lime slices to add interesting flavours. Vegetable juice is reviving and packed with vitamin goodness – cucumber and carrot are great for juicing, and they go well with fruit – such as apples – and herbs. Honey and maple syrup are good sweeteners for hot or cold drinks. Drinking plenty of water is also an important part of the cleansing routine. Consider purchasing a filter to save on the expense of repeatedly buying mineral water.

LIGHTER DAIRY OPTIONS

Light medium-fat soft goat's cheese is a tasty alternative to rich cream cheeses – mix it with a little chopped fresh mint and chives, then serve it in a little pot for the cheese course of a meal.

Small amounts of strong-flavoured cheese, such as Parmesan shavings, bring oodles of taste for a comparatively small amount of fat – use instead of a mild Cheddar, or other bland-tasting hard cheeses.

Feta, light mozzarella and ricotta cheeses are versatile for salads and appetizers – use them in small amounts with plenty of young salad leaves and spring vegetables.

Greek (US strained plain) yogurt is a creamy and delicious alternative to whipped cream for special occasions. Low-fat yogurt and virtually fat-free fromage frais are good everyday dairy products – use these to dress salads or freshly-cooked vegetables, adding a little seasoning and a handful of chopped herbs.

Drizzle a little walnut or macadamia nut oil over freshly cooked vegetables instead of using butter.

GRAINS AND SEEDS

Just as spring is the season for sowing seeds in the garden, it is also a good time for cooking with grains and seeds, and their products. For instance, cook with a mixture of brown, red and wild rice to add interesting texture and flavour to a dish.

Rolled oats are versatile in cooking, and are a delicious component of traditional breakfasts. Combined with a little grated cheese they make an excellent savoury topping for baked vegetable dishes. They are also a classic coating for oily fish – great for pan-frying or baking.

Oatcakes are made with oats and sometimes wheat. They are simple to serve and delicious with soups, pâtés and other appetizers, as well as with a cheese course.

Sprouted seeds are terrific spring salad ingredients – mung beans and alfalfa seeds in particular are crisp and delicious to eat.

Millet, buckwheat and quinoa are all versatile grains. Used cold, they add texture and bulk to fresh spring salads, and can be served hot as an alternative to rice or couscous.

Young and Crisp

As the days get longer and warmer, farmers' markets and local shops begin to stock a wider selection of mouthwatering spring produce. Enjoy first courses and side dishes that make the most of the new season's crisp shoots and tender herbs.

This delightful recipe transforms the classic wintry soup into a fresh-tasting and flavourful spring dish that is a celebration of these early vegetables.

SPRING MINESTRONE

INGREDIENTS
serves six

30ml | 2 tbsp olive oil

2 onions, finely chopped

2 garlic cloves, finely chopped

2 carrots, very finely chopped

1 celery stick, very finely chopped

1.3 litres | 2¼ pints | 5⅔ cups boiling water

450g | 1lb | 2½ cups shelled fresh broad (fava) beans

225g | 8oz mangetouts (snow peas), cut into fine strips

3 tomatoes, peeled and chopped

5ml | 1 tsp tomato purée (paste)

50g | 2oz spaghettini, broken into 4cm | 1½in lengths

225g | 8oz baby spinach

30ml | 2 tbsp chopped fresh parsley

handful of fresh basil leaves

salt and ground black pepper

sprigs of basil to garnish, and freshly grated Parmesan cheese to serve

1 Heat the oil in a pan and add the onions and garlic. Cook for 4–5 minutes, or until softened. Add the carrots and celery, and cook for 2–3 minutes. Add the boiling water and simmer for 15 minutes, or until the vegetables are tender.

2 Cook the broad beans in salted boiling water for 4–5 minutes. Remove with a slotted spoon, refresh under cold water and set aside.

3 Bring the pan of water back to the boil, add the mangetouts and cook for 1 minute. Drain, then refresh under cold water and set aside.

4 Add the tomatoes and the tomato purée to the soup. Cook for 1 minute. Purée two or three large ladlefuls of the soup and a quarter of the broad beans in a food processor or blender until smooth. Set aside.

5 Add the spaghettini to the remaining soup and cook for 6–8 minutes until tender. Stir in the purée and spinach and cook for 2–3 minutes. Add the rest of the broad beans, the mangetouts and parsley, and season well.

6 When you are ready to serve the soup, stir in the basil leaves and ladle the soup into deep cups or bowls. Garnish with sprigs of basil and serve with a little grated Parmesan.

The pointed, spear-shaped leaves of sorrel are one of the first wild salad greens to appear in spring. They make a refreshingly sharp chilled soup.

SORREL SOUP

1 Finely shred the sorrel, then put it in a large pan with the onion and stock. Bring to the boil, then reduce the heat and simmer for 10–15 minutes.

2 Add the sugar and half the lemon juice to the pan, stir and simmer for a further 5–10 minutes.

3 In a bowl, beat the eggs and mix in the sour cream, then stir in about 250ml|8fl oz| 1 cup of the hot soup. Add another 250ml|8fl oz|1 cup of soup, stirring as you go to ensure a smooth texture.

4 Slowly pour the egg mixture into the hot soup, stirring constantly to prevent the eggs curdling and to ensure the texture remains smooth. Cook for just a few moments over a low heat until the soup thickens slightly. Season with a little salt to taste and stir in the remaining lemon juice.

5 Leave the soup to cool, then chill for at least 2 hours. Taste again for seasoning (it may need more salt or lemon juice) and serve sprinkled with the spring onions.

COOK'S TIP Shred the sorrel across the grain. This will help to prevent it from becoming stringy when it is cooked.

INGREDIENTS
serves four to six

500g|1¹/₄lb sorrel leaves, stems removed

1 medium-large onion, thinly sliced

1.5 litres|2¹/₂ pints|6¹/₄ cups vegetable stock

15–30ml|1–2 tbsp sugar

60ml|4 tbsp lemon juice

2 eggs

150ml|¹/₄ pint|²/₃ cup sour cream

salt

3–4 spring onions (scallions), thinly sliced, to garnish

Lightly cumin-spiced rice makes a fragrant filling for stuffed vine leaves, which is perfectly complemented by the new season's mint. It makes an ideal first course for a springtime lunch or dinner.

STUFFED VINE LEAVES with CUMIN and MINT

INGREDIENTS
serves six to eight

250g | 9oz | 1¼ cups brown rice

30–45ml | 2–3 tbsp natural (plain) yogurt

3 garlic cloves, chopped

1 egg, lightly beaten

5–10ml | 1–2 tsp ground cumin

2.5ml | ½ tsp ground cinnamon

several handfuls of raisins

3–4 spring onions (scallions), thinly sliced

½ bunch fresh mint, plus extra to garnish

about 25 preserved or fresh vine leaves

salt, if necessary

8–10 unpeeled garlic cloves

juice of ½–1 lemon

90ml | 6 tbsp olive oil

for serving

1 lemon, cut into wedges or half slices

15–25 Greek black olives

150ml | ¼ pint | ⅔ cup natural yogurt

1 Put the rice in a pan with 300ml | ½ pint | 1¼ cups water. Bring to the boil, reduce the heat, cover and simmer for 30 minutes, or until just tender. Drain well and leave to cool.

2 Put the cooked rice in a bowl, add the yogurt, garlic, egg, ground cumin and cinnamon, raisins, spring onions and mint and mix together.

3 If you are using preserved vine leaves, rinse them well. If using fresh vine leaves, blanch in salted boiling water for 2–3 minutes, then rinse under cold water and drain.

4 Lay the leaves on a board, shiny side down. Place 15–30ml | 1–2 tbsp of the mixture near the stalk of each leaf. Fold each one up, starting at the bottom, then the sides, and finally rolling up towards the top to enclose the filling.

5 Carefully layer the rolls in a steamer and stud with the whole garlic cloves. Fill the base of the steamer with water and drizzle the lemon juice and olive oil evenly over the rolls. Cover the steamer tightly and cook over a medium-high heat for about 40 minutes, adding more water to the steamer if necessary.

6 Remove the steamer from the heat and set aside to cool slightly. Arrange the vine leaves on a serving dish and serve hot or, alternatively, leave to cool completely. Garnish and serve with lemon wedges or half slices, olives and a bowl of yogurt, for dipping.

VARIATIONS For a twist to the classic stuffed vine leaf, other herbs such as dill or parsley can be used, and a handful of pine nuts can be added to the stuffing.

As the first lettuces appear, this traditional French way of braising them with peas and spring onions in butter makes a light side dish that is perfect with simply cooked fish or roast or grilled duck.

BRAISED LETTUCE and PEAS with MINT

INGREDIENTS
serves four

50g | 2oz | 1/4 cup butter

4 Little Gem (Bibb) lettuces, halved lengthways

2 bunches spring onions (scallions), trimmed and halved

5ml | 1 tsp caster (superfine) sugar

400g | 14oz | 3 1/2 cups fresh shelled or frozen peas

4 fresh mint sprigs

120ml | 4fl oz | 1/2 cup chicken or vegetable stock or water

salt and ground black pepper

15ml | 1 tbsp chopped fresh mint to garnish

1 Melt half the butter in a wide, heavy pan over a low heat. Add the prepared lettuces and spring onions.

2 Turn the vegetables in the butter, then sprinkle in the sugar, 2.5ml | 1/2 tsp salt and plenty of black pepper. Cover and cook very gently for 5 minutes, stirring once.

3 Add the peas and mint sprigs. Turn the peas in the buttery juices and pour in the stock or water, then cover and cook over a gentle heat for a further 5 minutes. Uncover and increase the heat to reduce the liquid to a few tablespoons.

4 Stir in the remaining butter and adjust the seasoning. Transfer to a warmed serving dish and sprinkle with the chopped mint. Serve immediately.

VARIATIONS
• Braise about 250g | 9oz baby carrots with the lettuce.
• Use 1 lettuce, shredding it coarsely, and omit the mint. Towards the end of cooking, stir in about 150g | 5oz rocket (arugula) – preferably the stronger-flavoured wild rocket – and cook briefly until wilted.
• Fry 115g | 4oz chopped smoked bacon or pancetta with 1 small chopped onion in the butter. Use 1 bunch of spring onions and omit the mint. Stir in some chopped parsley before serving. This version is also very good with small turnips, braised with lettuce.

Make the most of fresh globe artichokes as soon as they are available by serving them with this delicious garlic and mayonnaise dressing from Spain.

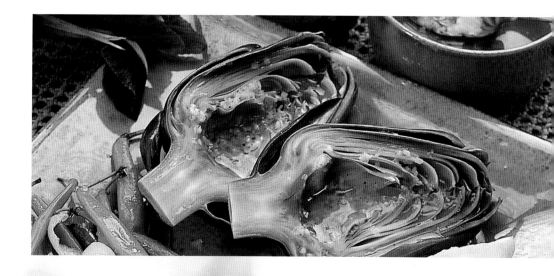

GLOBE ARTICHOKES with BEANS and AIOLI

1 First, make the aioli. Put the garlic and vinegar in a food processor or blender. With the motor running, slowly pour in the olive oil through the lid or feeder tube until the mixture is quite thick and smooth. (Alternatively, crush the garlic to a paste with the vinegar and gradually beat in the oil using a hand whisk.) Season with salt and pepper to taste.

2 Cook the green beans in lightly salted boiling water for 1–2 minutes, or until slightly softened. Drain well.

3 Trim the artichoke stalks close to the base. Cook the artichokes in a large pan of salted water for about 30 minutes, or until you can easily pull away a leaf from the base. Drain well.

4 Using a large, sharp knife, cut the artichokes in half lengthways and carefully scrape out the hairy choke using a teaspoon.

5 Arrange the artichokes and beans on serving plates and drizzle with the olive oil. Sprinkle the lemon rind over them and season to taste with coarse salt and a little pepper. Spoon the aioli into the artichoke hearts and serve the dish warm, garnished with lemon wedges.

6 To eat the artichokes, squeeze a little lemon juice over them, then pull the leaves from the base one at a time and use to scoop a little of the aioli sauce. Gently scrape away the fleshy end of each leaf with your teeth and discard the remainder of the leaf. Eat the tender base or "heart" of the artichoke with a knife and fork.

INGREDIENTS
serves three

225g | 8oz green beans

3 small globe artichokes

15ml | 1 tbsp olive oil

pared rind of 1 lemon

coarse salt, for sprinkling

lemon wedges, to garnish

for the aioli

6 large garlic cloves, thinly sliced

10ml | 2 tsp white wine vinegar

250ml | 8fl oz | 1 cup olive oil

salt and ground black pepper

As spring progresses towards summer, we look for lighter first courses and side dishes. The new season's asparagus is an ideal choice served with a tangy lemon and egg sauce.

ASPARAGUS with LEMON SAUCE

1 Cook the bundle of asparagus in salted boiling water for 7–10 minutes.

2 Drain well and arrange the asparagus in a serving dish. Reserve 200ml|7fl oz| scant 1 cup of the cooking liquid.

3 Blend the cornflour with the cooled, reserved cooking liquid and place in a small pan. Bring to the boil, stirring constantly, and cook over a gentle heat until the sauce thickens slightly. Stir in the sugar, then remove the pan from the heat and allow to cool slightly.

4 Beat the egg yolks thoroughly with the lemon juice and stir gradually into the cooled sauce. Cook over a very low heat, stirring constantly, until the sauce is fairly thick. Be careful not to overheat the sauce or it may curdle. As soon as the sauce has thickened, remove the pan from the heat and continue stirring for 1 minute. Taste and add salt or sugar as necessary. Allow the sauce to cool slightly.

5 Stir the cooled sauce, then pour a little over the asparagus. Cover and chill for at least 2 hours before serving with the rest of the sauce.

VARIATIONS This sauce goes very well with all sorts of young vegetables. Try it with baby leeks, cooked whole or chopped, or serve it with other baby vegetables, such as carrots and courgettes (zucchini).

COOK'S TIP Use tiny asparagus spears for an elegant first course or a dinner party.

INGREDIENTS
serves four

675g|1¹/₂lb asparagus, tough ends removed, and tied in a bundle

15ml|1 tbsp cornflour (cornstarch)

about 10ml|2 tsp sugar

2 egg yolks

juice of 1¹/₂ lemons

salt

Light and Fresh

After comforting and substantial winter fare, we look
forward to cleaner flavours, buying what is plentiful and
cooking in new and imaginative ways. These light meals and
salads are designed for easy, one-course eating that will
fit in with an active lifestyle.

Full of flavour, this easily prepared omelette makes a superb lunch or light supper and uses many of the season's ingredients.

SPRING VEGETABLE OMELETTE

INGREDIENTS
serves four

50g | 2oz | 1/2 cup fresh asparagus tips

50g | 2oz spring greens (collards), shredded

15ml | 1 tbsp sunflower oil

1 onion, sliced

175g | 6oz cooked new potatoes, halved or diced

2 tomatoes, chopped

6 eggs

15–30ml | 1–2 tbsp chopped fresh mixed herbs

salt and ground black pepper

salad, to serve

1 Steam the asparagus tips and spring greens over a pan of boiling water for 5–10 minutes, until tender. Drain the vegetables and keep them warm.

2 Heat the oil in a large frying pan that can safely be used under the grill (broiler). (Cover a wooden handle with foil to protect it.) Add the onion and cook over a low heat, stirring occasionally, for 5–10 minutes, until softened.

3 Add the new potatoes and cook, stirring constantly, for 3 minutes. Stir in the tomatoes, asparagus and spring greens. Beat the eggs lightly with the herbs and season to taste with salt and pepper.

4 Preheat the grill. Pour the egg mixture over the vegetables, then cook over a gentle heat until the base of the omelette is golden brown. Slide the pan under the grill and cook the omelette for 2–3 minutes, or until the top is golden brown. Serve immediately, cut into wedges, with salad.

White wine melds the flavours of bacon, spring greens and alliums in this light, spring dish. Serve with some crusty bread.

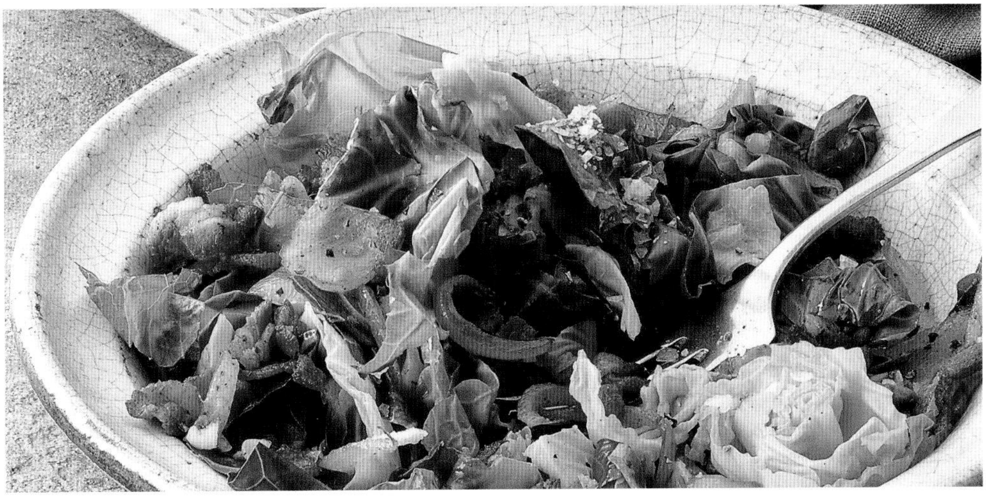

SPRING GREENS with BACON

1 In a large frying pan, heat the oil and butter and add the bacon. Fry for 2 minutes, then add the onions and fry for another 3 minutes, or until the onion begins to soften.

2 Add the wine and simmer vigorously for 2 minutes to reduce the liquid.

3 Reduce the heat and add the garlic, spring greens and salt and pepper. Cook over a low heat for about 15 minutes, or until the greens are tender. (Cover the pan so that the greens retain their colour.) Serve hot.

VARIATIONS If spring greens are difficult to get hold of, try other greens. Crisp curly kale or red or green cabbage will work well in this recipe. They may need a little longer cooking time and would stand up to a red wine.
- Likewise red or green chard, with its firm stems, or young spinach will do well but requires only the lightest cooking.
- Try this with mangetouts (snow peas) and white wine served with fresh, hot pasta.
- For a dinner party side dish, replace the bacon with chunks of pancetta.

INGREDIENTS
serves four

30ml | 2 tbsp olive oil

30ml | 2 tbsp butter

4 rashers (strips) bacon, chopped

1 large onion, thinly sliced

250ml | 8fl oz | 1 cup dry white wine

2 garlic cloves, finely chopped

900g | 2lb spring greens (collards), shredded

salt and ground black pepper

These melt-in-the-mouth herby spring onion fritters are excellent served with a fresh spicy salsa made with avocados, red onion and chilli.

RICOTTA and HERB FRITTERS

INGREDIENTS
serves four

250g | 9oz | generous 1 cup ricotta cheese

1 large (US extra large) egg, beaten

90ml | 6 tbsp self-raising (self-rising) flour

90ml | 6 tbsp milk

1 bunch spring onions (scallions), finely sliced

30ml | 2 tbsp chopped fresh coriander (cilantro)

sunflower oil, for shallow frying

salt and ground black pepper

200ml | 7fl oz | scant 1 cup crème fraîche, to serve

fresh coriander sprigs and lime wedges, to garnish

fresh salsa, to serve

1 Beat the ricotta until smooth, then beat in the egg and flour, followed by the milk to make a smooth, thick batter. Beat in the spring onions and coriander. Season well with pepper and a little salt.

2 Heat a little oil in a non-stick frying pan over a medium heat. Add spoonfuls of the mixture to make fritters about 7.5cm | 3in across and fry for about 4–5 minutes each side, or until set and browned. The mixture makes 12 fritters.

3 Serve the fritters immediately, with salsa and a dollop of crème fraîche. Garnish with coriander sprigs and lime wedges.

COOK'S TIP Make a quick salsa by finely chopping avocado, red onion and fresh tomatoes. Add red chilli to taste and the juice and rind of a lime. Taste the salsa and adjust the seasoning, adding more lime juice and/or sugar to taste. You might like to add one or two teaspoons of Thai fish sauce if you have some. Leave for 30 minutes for the flavours to develop.

VARIATION The fritters are also good served with thinly sliced smoked salmon.

Grilling late-spring vegetables gives them a slight smokiness that goes very well with the sweetness of air-dried ham. Shaved Pecorino cheese adds a final flourish to the delicious flavours.

GRILLED GREENS with HAM and CHEESE

1 Cut off and discard the woody ends of the asparagus and use a vegetable peeler to peel the bottom 7.5cm|3in of the spears.

2 Preheat the grill (broiler). Toss the spring onions and asparagus in 30ml|2 tbsp of the oil. Place on two baking sheets and season with salt and pepper.

3 Grill (broil) the asparagus for 5 minutes on each side, or until just tender when tested with the tip of a sharp knife. Protect the tips with foil if they seem to char too much. Grill the spring onions for about 3–4 minutes on each side, or until tinged with brown. Brush both vegetables with more oil when you turn them.

4 Distribute the vegetables among four to six plates. Season with pepper, and drizzle over the vinegar. Lay two to three slices of ham on each plate and shave the Pecorino cheese over the top. Serve more extra virgin olive oil for drizzling at the table.

COOK'S TIPS The spring onions can be cooked on a cast-iron ridged griddle. If more convenient, the asparagus can be roasted at 200°C|400°F|Gas 6 for 15 minutes.

INGREDIENTS
serves four to six

500g | 1¼lb asparagus

2 bunches plump spring onions (scallions) (about 24)

45–60ml | 3–4 tbsp extra virgin olive oil

20ml | 4 tsp balsamic vinegar

8–12 slices prosciutto or San Daniele ham

50g | 2oz Pecorino cheese

salt and ground black pepper

extra virgin olive oil, to serve

A richly flavoured tomato sauce with garlic, fennel and artichokes makes a fine accompaniment for penne. This is the perfect dish to serve when globe artichokes are in season.

ARTICHOKES with PENNE

INGREDIENTS
serves six

juice of 1 lemon

2 globe artichokes

30ml | 2 tbsp olive oil

1 small fennel bulb, thinly sliced, with feathery tops reserved

1 onion, finely chopped

4 garlic cloves, finely chopped

1 handful fresh flat leaf parsley, coarsely chopped

400g | 14oz can chopped plum tomatoes

150ml | 1/4 pint | 2/3 cup dry white wine

350g | 12oz | 3 cups dried penne

10ml | 2 tsp capers, chopped

salt and ground black pepper

freshly grated Parmesan cheese, to serve

1 Fill a large mixing bowl with cold water and add half the lemon juice. To prepare the artichokes, cut or break off the stalks, then pull off and discard the outer leaves until only the pale inner leaves remain. Cut off the tops of these leaves, cut the base in half lengthways, then prise the hairy choke out of the centre with the tip of the knife and discard. Cut the artichoke lengthways into 5mm | 1/4in pieces, adding them immediately to the bowl of acidulated water to prevent them discolouring.

2 Bring a large pan of salted water to the boil. Drain the artichokes and add them immediately to the water. Boil for 5 minutes, then drain and set aside. Heat the oil in a large pan and add the fennel, onion, garlic and parsley. Cook over a low to medium heat, stirring frequently, for 10 minutes, or until the fennel has softened and is lightly coloured.

3 Add the tomatoes and wine, with seasoning to taste. Bring to the boil, stirring, then lower the heat, cover and simmer for 10–15 minutes. Stir in the artichokes, replace the lid and simmer for 10 minutes more. Meanwhile, add the pasta to a large pan of lightly salted boiling water and cook according to the instructions on the packet.

4 Drain the pasta, reserving a little of the cooking water. Add the capers to the sauce, stir well then taste for seasoning. Add the remaining lemon juice. Tip the pasta into a warmed serving bowl, pour the sauce over and toss thoroughly to mix, adding a little of the reserved cooking water if you like a thinner sauce. Serve immediately, garnished with the reserved fennel fronds. Hand around a bowl of grated Parmesan separately.

Baby spinach leaves and creamy avocado are given a sharp tang by the simple lemon dressing in this refreshing spring salad with crunchy polenta croûtons.

SPINACH and AVOCADO SALAD

1 Preheat the oven to 200°C | 400°F | Gas 6. Place the onion wedges and polenta cubes on a lightly oiled baking sheet and bake for 25 minutes, or until the onion is tender and the polenta is crisp and golden, turning them regularly to prevent them sticking. Leave to cool slightly.

2 Meanwhile, make the dressing. Place the olive oil, lemon juice and seasoning to taste in a bowl or screw-top jar. Stir or shake thoroughly to combine.

3 Place the spinach leaves in a serving bowl. Toss the avocado in the lemon juice to prevent it browning, then add to the spinach with the roasted onions.

4 Pour the dressing over the salad and toss gently to combine. Sprinkle the polenta croûtons on top or hand them round separately, and serve immediately.

COOK'S TIP If you can't find ready-made polenta, you can make your own using instant polenta grains. Simply cook according to the packet instructions, then pour into a tray and leave to cool and set.

INGREDIENTS
serves four

1 large red onion, cut into wedges

350g | 12oz ready-made polenta, cut into 1cm | 1/2in cubes

olive oil, for brushing

225g | 8oz baby spinach leaves

1 avocado, peeled, stoned (pitted) and sliced

5ml | 1 tsp lemon juice

for the dressing

60ml | 4 tbsp extra virgin olive oil

juice of 1/2 lemon

salt and ground black pepper

As late spring days become warmer, it may feel too hot for big pasta dishes. Try serving tagliatelle as a warm salad combined with ham, eggs and asparagus.

WARM TAGLIATELLE SALAD with ASPARAGUS

INGREDIENTS
serves four

450g | 1lb asparagus

450g | 1lb dried tagliatelle

225g | 8oz cooked ham, in 5mm | ¼in thick slices, cut into fingers

2 eggs, hard-boiled and sliced

50g | 2oz Parmesan cheese, shaved

salt and ground black pepper

for the dressing

50g | 2oz cooked potato

75ml | 5 tbsp olive oil

15ml | 1 tbsp lemon juice

10ml | 2 tsp Dijon mustard

120ml | 4fl oz | ½ cup vegetable stock

1 Trim and discard the tough woody part of the asparagus. Cut the spears in half and cook the thicker halves in salted boiling water for 12 minutes. After 6 minutes add the tips. Drain, then refresh under cold water until warm.

2 Finely chop 150g | 5oz of the thick asparagus pieces. Place in a food processor with the dressing ingredients and process until smooth.

3 Boil the pasta in a large pan of salted water according to the packet instructions until tender. Refresh under cold water until warm, and drain.

4 To serve, toss the pasta with the asparagus sauce and divide among four pasta plates. Top with the ham, hard-boiled eggs and asparagus tips. Serve with a sprinkling of Parmesan cheese shavings.

VARIATIONS Use sliced chicken instead of the ham, or thin slices of softer Italian cheese, such as Fontina or Asiago.

Tender and Tasty

From spring lamb and chicken to Dover sole and
scallops, there is a wide selection of good-quality meat,
fish and poultry available at this
time of year. Instead of hunting for a particular
ingredient, take advantage of what is plentiful and use
whatever looks good and fresh in the shops.

For a light springtime meal, try crisply coated plaice or flounder served with a simple tomato sauce. It makes a delicious choice for a family supper.

FRIED FISH with TOMATO SAUCE

INGREDIENTS
serves four

25g | 1oz | 1/4 cup plain (all-purpose) flour

2 eggs, beaten

75g | 3oz | generous 1 cup dried breadcrumbs, preferably home-made

4 small plaice or flounder, skin removed

15g | 1/2oz | 1 tbsp butter

15ml | 1 tbsp sunflower oil

salt and ground black pepper

1 lemon, quartered, to serve

fresh basil leaves, to garnish

for the sauce

30ml | 2 tbsp olive oil

1 red onion, finely chopped

1 garlic clove, finely chopped

400g | 14oz can chopped tomatoes

15ml | 1 tbsp tomato purée (paste)

15ml | 1 tbsp torn fresh basil leaves

1 First make the tomato sauce. Heat the olive oil in a large pan, add the finely chopped onion and garlic and cook gently for about 5 minutes, or until softened and pale golden. Stir in the chopped tomatoes and tomato purée and simmer for 20–30 minutes, stirring occasionally. Season with salt and pepper and stir in the basil.

2 Spread out the flour in a shallow dish, pour the beaten eggs into another and spread out the breadcrumbs in a third. Season the plaice or flounder with salt and pepper.

3 Hold a fish in your left hand and dip first in flour, then in egg and finally in the breadcrumbs, patting the crumbs on with your dry right hand.

4 Heat the butter and oil in a frying pan until foaming. Fry the fish one at a time in the hot fat for about 5 minutes on each side, or until golden brown and cooked through but still juicy in the middle. Drain on kitchen paper and keep hot while you fry the rest. Serve with lemon wedges and the tomato sauce, garnished with basil leaves.

VARIATIONS This recipe works equally well with lemon sole or dabs (these do not need skinning), or fillets of haddock and whiting.

Thai flavourings add a new dimension to the delicate taste and texture of Dover sole. Lightly steamed in lettuce and accompanied by mussels, it makes a tasty and unusual dish.

STEAMED LETTUCE-WRAPPED SOLE

INGREDIENTS
serves four

2 large Dover or lemon sole fillets, skinned

15ml | 1 tbsp sesame seeds

15ml | 1 tbsp sunflower or groundnut (peanut) oil

10ml | 2 tsp sesame oil

2.5cm | 1in piece fresh root ginger, peeled and grated

3 garlic cloves, finely chopped

15ml | 1 tbsp soy sauce or Thai fish sauce

juice of 1 lemon

2 spring onions (scallions), thinly sliced

8 large soft lettuce leaves

12 large fresh mussels, scrubbed and bearded

1 Cut the sole fillets in half lengthways. Season and set aside. Prepare a steamer.

2 Heat a heavy frying pan until hot. Toast the sesame seeds lightly and set aside.

3 Heat the oils in the frying pan over a medium heat. Add the ginger and garlic and cook until lightly coloured. Stir in the soy sauce or Thai fish sauce, lemon juice and spring onions. Remove from the heat, and stir in the sesame seeds.

4 Lay the pieces of fish on baking parchment, skinned side up. Spread each evenly with the ginger mixture. Roll up each piece, starting at the tail end. Place on a baking sheet.

5 Plunge the lettuce leaves into the boiling water you have prepared for the steamer and immediately lift them out with tongs or a slotted spoon. Lay them out flat on kitchen paper and gently pat them dry. Wrap each sole parcel in two lettuce leaves, making sure that the filling is well covered to keep it in place.

6 Arrange the fish parcels in a steamer basket. Cover and steam over simmering water for 8 minutes. Discard any opened mussels that do not close when sharply tapped. Add the mussels, and steam for 2–4 minutes, or until opened. Discard any that remain closed. Put the parcels on individual warmed plates, halve and garnish with mussels. Serve immediately.

VARIATION Trout, plaice, flounder or brill are all excellent cooked this way.

This Jewish dish of fresh tuna and peas is enjoyed in Italy at Pesach (Passover), which falls in spring, served with matzo pancakes. Garlic, parsley and a hint of fennel give the tuna an unusual and appetizing flavour.

TONNO CON PISELLI

1 Preheat the oven to 190°C|375°F|Gas 5. Heat the olive oil in a large frying pan, then add the chopped onion, garlic, flat leaf parsley and fennel seeds, and fry over a low heat for about 5 minutes, or until the onion is softened but not browned.

2 Sprinkle the tuna steaks on each side with salt and pepper. Add to the pan and cook for 2–3 minutes on each side, or until lightly browned. Transfer the tuna steaks to a shallow baking dish, in a single layer.

3 Add the canned tomatoes along with their juice and the wine or fish stock to the onions and cook over a medium heat for 5–10 minutes, stirring, until the flavours blend together and the mixture thickens slightly.

4 Stir the tomato purée, sugar, if needed, and salt and pepper into the tomato sauce, then add the fresh or frozen peas. Pour the mixture over the fish steaks and bake, uncovered, for about 10 minutes, or until tender. Serve with traditional matzo pancakes or use pitta or another flatbread.

VARIATIONS Use tuna fillets in place of the steaks or try different fish steaks, such as salmon or swordfish.

INGREDIENTS
serves four

60ml | 4 tbsp olive oil

1 onion, chopped

4–5 garlic cloves, chopped

45ml | 3 tbsp chopped fresh flat leaf parsley

1–2 pinches of fennel seeds

350g | 12oz tuna steaks

400g | 14oz can chopped tomatoes

120ml | 4fl oz | 1/2 cup dry white wine or fish stock

30–45ml | 2–3 tbsp tomato purée (paste)

pinch of sugar, if needed

350g | 12oz | 3 cups fresh shelled peas

salt and ground black pepper

Scallops are one of the most delicious shellfish and are available throughout the spring. Here they are partnered with a delicious chive sauce and a pilaff of wild and white rice with sweet leeks and carrots.

SCALLOPS with LEEK and CARROT RICE

1 Lightly season the scallops, brush with 15ml | 1 tbsp of the olive oil and set aside. Cook the wild rice in plenty of boiling water for about 30 minutes, or until tender, then drain.

2 Melt half the butter in a small frying pan and cook the carrots gently for 4–5 minutes. Add the leeks and fry for another 2 minutes. Season and add 30–45ml | 2–3 tbsp water, then cover and cook for a few minutes more. Uncover and cook until the liquid has reduced. Remove from the heat.

3 Melt half the remaining butter with 15ml | 1 tbsp of the remaining oil in a heavy pan. Add the onion and fry for 3–4 minutes, or until softened but not browned. Add the long grain rice and bay leaf and cook, stirring constantly, until the rice looks translucent and the grains are coated with oil.

4 Pour in half the wine and stock. Add 2.5ml | 1/2 tsp salt and bring to the boil. Stir, then cover and cook gently for 15 minutes, or until the liquid is absorbed and the rice is tender. Reheat the carrots and leeks, then stir them into the long grain rice with the wild rice. Adjust the seasoning.

5 Pour the remaining wine and stock into a small pan and boil rapidly until reduced by half. Heat a heavy frying pan over a high heat. Add the remaining butter and oil. Sear the scallops for 1–2 minutes each side, then set aside and keep warm.

6 Pour the reduced stock into the pan and heat until bubbling, then add the cream and boil until thickened. Season and add lemon juice, chives and scallops. Stir the chervil into the rice. Serve the rice with the scallops on top and spoon the sauce over.

INGREDIENTS
serves four

12–16 shelled scallops

45ml | 3 tbsp olive oil

50g | 2oz | 1/3 cup wild rice

65g | 2 1/2 oz | 5 tbsp butter

4 carrots, cut into long thin strips

2 leeks, cut into thick, diagonal slices

1 small onion, finely chopped

115g | 4oz | 2/3 cup long grain rice

1 fresh bay leaf

200ml | 7fl oz | scant 1 cup white wine

450ml | 3/4 pint | scant 2 cups fish stock

60ml | 4 tbsp double (heavy) cream

a little lemon juice

25ml | 1 1/2 tbsp chopped fresh chives

30ml | 2 tbsp chervil sprigs

salt and ground black pepper

A lovely wine and herb-scented stock contains tender morsels of chicken and baby vegetables in this light and aromatic seasonal version of the French casserole.

CHICKEN POT AU FEU

INGREDIENTS
serves four

1 chicken, about 2.25kg | 5lb

1 parsley sprig

15ml | 1 tbsp black peppercorns

1 bay leaf

300g | 11oz baby carrots, washed and left whole

175g | 6oz baby leeks, washed and left whole

25g | 1oz | 2 tbsp butter

15ml | 1 tbsp olive oil

300g | 11oz shallots, halved if large

200ml | 7fl oz | scant 1 cup dry white wine

800g | 1³/₄lb baby new potatoes

120ml | 4fl oz | ¹/₂ cup double (heavy) cream

salt and ground black pepper

small bunch parsley or tarragon, chopped, to garnish

1 Joint the chicken into eight pieces and place the carcass in a large stockpot. Add the parsley sprig, peppercorns, bay leaf and the trimmings from the carrots and leeks. Cover with cold water and bring to the boil. Simmer for 45 minutes, then strain.

2 Meanwhile, melt the butter with the olive oil in a frying pan, then add the chicken pieces. Add seasoning, and brown the chicken all over. Transfer the chicken pieces to a plate and add the shallots to the pan. Cook over a low heat for 20 minutes, stirring occasionally, until softened, but not browned.

3 Return the chicken to the pan and add the wine. Scoop up any juices from the base of the pan with a wooden spoon, then add the carrots, leeks and potatoes with enough stock to just cover. Bring to the boil, then cover and simmer for 20 minutes. Stir in the cream.

4 Transfer to a serving dish and garnish with the herbs. Serve immediately.

Tender poussins are spatchcocked and grilled with a garlic and spring herb butter, making this a light and extremely tasty dish that is quick to cook.

SPATCHCOCK POUSSINS with SPRING HERBS

INGREDIENTS
serves two

2 poussins, each weighing about 450g | 1lb

1 shallot, finely chopped

2 garlic cloves, crushed

45ml | 3 tbsp chopped mixed fresh herbs, such as flat leaf parsley, sage, rosemary and thyme

75g | 3oz | 6 tbsp butter, softened

salt and ground black pepper

1 To spatchcock a poussin, place it breast down on a chopping board and split it along the back. Open out the bird and turn it over, so that the breast side is uppermost. Press the bird as flat as possible, then thread two metal skewers through it, across the breast and thigh, to keep it flat. Repeat with the second poussin and place the skewered birds on a large grill (broiling) pan.

2 Add the chopped shallot, crushed garlic and chopped mixed herbs to the butter with plenty of seasoning, and then beat well. Dot the butter over the spatchcock poussins.

3 Preheat the grill (broiler) to high and cook the poussins for 30 minutes, turning them over halfway through. Turn again and baste with the cooking juices, then cook for a further 5–7 minutes on each side.

VARIATIONS The addition of some finely chopped chilli or a little grated lemon rind to the butter will give it a lift.

Mild, sweet leeks and tender baby vegetables are excellent braised in wine with prime guinea fowl flavoured with mustard and mint.

GUINEA FOWL with BABY VEGETABLES

1 Heat 30ml | 2 tbsp of the oil in a large frying pan and cook the pancetta over a medium heat until lightly browned, stirring occasionally. Remove the pancetta and set aside.

2 Season the flour with salt and pepper and toss the guinea fowl portions in it. Fry in the oil remaining in the pan until browned on all sides. Transfer to a flameproof casserole. Preheat the oven to 180°C | 350°F | Gas 4.

3 Add the remaining oil to the pan and cook the onion gently until soft. Add the garlic and fry for 3–4 minutes, then stir in the pancetta and wine. Tie the thyme, bay leaf and parsley into a bundle and add to the pan. Bring to the boil, then simmer gently for 3–4 minutes. Pour over the guinea fowl in the casserole dish and add seasoning. Cover and cook in the oven for 40 minutes.

4 Add the baby carrots and turnips to the casserole and cook, covered, for another 30 minutes, or until the vegetables are just tender. Stir in the leeks and cook for a further 15–20 minutes, or until all the vegetables are fully cooked.

5 Meanwhile, blanch the peas in boiling water for 2 minutes, then drain. Transfer the guinea fowl and vegetables to a warmed serving dish. Place the casserole on the hob and boil the juices vigorously over a high heat until they are reduced by about half.

6 Stir in the peas and cook gently for 2–3 minutes, then stir in the mustard and adjust the seasoning. Stir in most of the parsley and the mint. Pour this sauce over the guinea fowl, scatter the remaining parsley over the top and serve immediately.

INGREDIENTS
serves four

45ml | 3 tbsp olive oil

115g | 4oz pancetta, cut into lardons

30ml | 2 tbsp plain (all-purpose) flour

2 1.2–1.6kg | 2¹/₂–3¹/₂lb guinea fowl, each jointed into 4 portions

1 onion, chopped

1 head of garlic, separated into cloves and peeled

1 bottle dry white wine

fresh thyme sprig

1 fresh bay leaf

a few parsley stalks

250g | 9oz baby carrots

250g | 9oz baby turnips

6 slender leeks, cut into 7.5cm | 3in lengths

250g | 9oz | 2¹/₄ cups fresh shelled peas

15ml | 1 tbsp French herb mustard

15g | ¹/₂oz | ¹/₄ cup chopped flat leaf parsley

15ml | 1 tbsp chopped fresh mint

salt and ground black pepper

Prepare this classic Greek dish when young lamb is at its best and lettuces and fresh dill are available. The unusual flavours make it an ideal choice for a dinner party, and it can also be cooked in advance.

COS LETTUCE and LAMB CASSEROLE

1 Heat the olive oil in a large, heavy pan. Add the chopped onion and sauté for 3–5 minutes, or until it glistens and becomes translucent.

2 Increase the heat, then add the lamb steaks and cook, turning them over frequently, until all the moisture has been driven off, a process that will take about 15 minutes.

3 Add salt to taste and enough hot water to cover the meat. Cover the pan and simmer for about 1 hour, until the meat is only just tender.

4 Add the lettuces, spring onions and dill. If necessary, pour in a little more hot water so that all the vegetables are almost covered. Replace the lid on the pan and simmer for 15–20 minutes more. Remove from the heat and let the dish stand for 5 minutes while you prepare the ingredients for the sauce.

5 Beat the eggs lightly in a bowl, add the cornflour mixture and beat until smooth. Add the lemon juice and whisk briefly, then continue to whisk while gradually adding 75–90ml/5–6 tbsp of the hot liquid from the pan containing the lamb.

6 Pour the sauce over the meat. Do not stir; instead gently shake and rotate the pan until the sauce is incorporated with the remaining liquid. Return the pan to a gentle heat for 2–3 minutes, just long enough to warm the sauce through. Do not let it boil, or the sauce is likely to curdle. Serve on warmed plates and scatter over some extra chopped dill.

INGREDIENTS
serves four to six

45ml | 3 tbsp olive oil

1 onion, chopped

1kg | 2¹/₄lb boned leg of lamb, sliced into 4–6 medium steaks

2 cos or romaine lettuces, coarsely shredded

6 spring onions (scallions), sliced

60ml | 4 tbsp roughly chopped fresh dill, plus extra to garnish (optional)

for the sauce

2 eggs

15ml | 1 tbsp cornflour (cornstarch), mixed to a paste with 120ml | 4fl oz | ¹/₂ cup water

juice of 1 lemon

salt

Fresh herbs and garlic add depth of flavour to this rack of lamb, which is served with Puy lentils in a rich tomato sauce. Serve with potatoes and steamed spring vegetables.

HERB-CRUSTED RACK of LAMB

INGREDIENTS
serves four

2 six-bone racks of lamb, chined

50g | 2oz | 1 cup fresh white breadcrumbs

2 large garlic cloves, crushed

90ml | 6 tbsp chopped mixed fresh herbs, such as rosemary, thyme, flat leaf parsley and marjoram, plus extra sprigs to garnish

50g | 2oz | ¼ cup butter, melted

salt and ground black pepper

new potatoes, to serve

for the Puy lentils

1 red onion, chopped

30ml | 2 tbsp olive oil

400g | 14oz can Puy or green lentils, rinsed and drained

400g | 14oz can chopped tomatoes

30ml | 2 tbsp chopped fresh parsley

1 Preheat the oven to 220°C | 425°F | Gas 7. Trim any excess fat from the lamb, season well with salt and pepper.

2 Mix together the breadcrumbs, garlic, herbs and butter, and press on to the fat side of the lamb. Place in a roasting pan and roast for 25 minutes. Cover with foil, and allow to stand for 5 minutes before carving.

3 To make the Puy lentils, cook the onion in the olive oil until softened. Add the lentils and tomatoes and cook gently for 5 minutes, or until the lentils are piping hot. Stir in the parsley and season to taste.

4 Cut each rack of lamb in half and serve with the lentils and new potatoes. Garnish with herb sprigs.

Sweet and Tart

Here are cakes and desserts that make the most of the
clean, sharp-tasting seasonal goodies.
Some treats like rhubarb have a very short season so
enjoy those tender pink shoots while you can.
More fruit than you can eat? Then preserve it by making
ice cream to enjoy later in the year.

Tender, slow-cooked orange gives this moist cake its fragrance. Serve with coffee, afternoon tea or with whipped cream for a perfect springtime dessert.

MOIST ORANGE and ALMOND CAKE

INGREDIENTS
serves eight

1 large Valencia or Navelina orange

butter, for greasing

3 eggs

225g | 8oz | generous 1 cup caster (superfine) sugar

5ml | 1 tsp baking powder

225g | 8oz | 2 cups ground almonds

25g | 1oz | ¼ cup plain (all-purpose) flour

icing (confectioners') sugar, for dusting

1 Pierce the orange with a skewer. Put it in a deep pan and pour over water to cover it. Bring to the boil, then cover and simmer for 1 hour until the skin is soft. Drain, then cool.

2 Preheat the oven to 180°C | 350°F | Gas 4. Lightly grease a 20cm | 8in round cake tin (pan) and line it with baking parchment. Cut the cooled orange in half and discard all the pips (seeds). Place the orange, peel, skin and all, in a food processor or blender and purée until smooth and pulpy.

3 In a bowl, whisk the eggs and caster sugar until thick. Fold in the baking powder, almonds and flour. Fold in the purée.

4 Pour into the prepared tin, level the surface and bake for 1 hour, or until a skewer inserted into the middle comes out clean. Cool the cake in the tin for 10 minutes, then turn out on to a wire rack, peel off the lining paper and cool completely. Dust the top liberally with icing sugar and serve.

COOK'S TIP To make a delicious dessert, tuck orange slices underneath the cake just before serving with whipped cream.

The sharp tang of spring rhubarb with this sweet meringue topping will really tantalize the taste buds. Delicious hot or cold with cream or vanilla ice cream.

RHUBARB MERINGUE PIE

1 Sift the flour into a bowl and add the ground walnuts. Rub in the butter until the mixture resembles very fine breadcrumbs. Stir in 30ml|2 tbsp of the sugar with 1 egg yolk beaten with 15ml|1 tbsp water. Mix to a firm dough. Turn out on to a floured surface and knead lightly. Wrap in a plastic bag and chill for at least 30 minutes.

2 Preheat the oven to 190°C|375°F|Gas 5. Roll out the pastry on a lightly floured surface and use to line a 23cm|9in fluted flan tin (tart pan). Prick the base with a fork. Line the pastry with baking parchment and fill with baking beans. Bake for 15 minutes.

3 Meanwhile, put the rhubarb, 75g|3oz|6 tbsp of the remaining sugar and the orange rind in a pan. Cover with a lid and cook over a low heat until the rhubarb is tender.

4 Remove the beans and paper from the pastry case, then brush all over with a little of the remaining egg yolk. Bake for 10–15 minutes, or until the pastry is crisp.

5 Blend together the cornflour and the orange juice in a small bowl. Remove from the heat, stir the cornflour mixture into the cooked rhubarb, then bring to the boil, stirring constantly until thickened. Cook for a further 1–2 minutes. Cool slightly, then beat in the remaining egg yolks. Pour into the flan case.

6 Whisk the egg whites until they form soft peaks, then whisk in the remaining sugar, 15ml|1 tbsp at time, whisking well after each addition.

7 Swirl the meringue over the filling to cover completely. Bake for 25 minutes, or until golden. Serve warm, or leave to cool, and serve with whipped cream.

INGREDIENTS
serves six

200g|7oz|1³/₄ cups plain (all-purpose) flour, plus extra for dusting

25g|1oz|¹/₄ cup ground walnuts

115g|4oz|¹/₂ cup butter, diced

275g|10oz|1¹/₂ cups caster (superfine) sugar

4 egg yolks

675g|1¹/₂lb rhubarb, cut into small pieces

finely grated rind and juice of 3 blood or navel oranges

75ml|5 tbsp cornflour (cornstarch)

3 egg whites

whipped cream, to serve

Use fresh free-range eggs with golden yolks for this tart if you can, as their colour will add to the look of the finished dessert.
It is very lemony, so serve with cream or vanilla ice.

CLASSIC LEMON TART

INGREDIENTS
serves eight

150g | 5oz | 1¼ cups plain (all-purpose) flour, sifted

50g | 2oz | ½ cup hazelnuts, toasted and finely ground

175g | 6oz | scant 1 cup caster (superfine) sugar

115g | 4oz | ½ cup unsalted (sweet) butter, softened

4 eggs

finely grated rind of 2 lemons and at least 175ml | 6fl oz | ¾ cup lemon juice

150ml | ¼ pint | ⅔ cup double (heavy) cream

1 Mix together the flour, nuts and 25g | 1oz | 2 tbsp sugar, then gently work in the butter and, if necessary, 15–30ml | 1–2 tbsp cold water to make a soft dough. Chill for 10 minutes. Roll out the dough and use to line a 20cm | 8in loose-based flan tin (tart pan). If you find it too difficult to roll out, push the pastry into the flan tin. Chill for about 20 minutes. Preheat the oven to 200°C | 400°F | Gas 6.

2 Line the pastry case with baking parchment, fill with baking beans, and bake for 15 minutes. Remove the paper and beans, and cook for a further 5–10 minutes, or until the base is crisp.

3 Beat the eggs, lemon rind and juice, the remaining sugar and cream until well blended. Pour into the pastry case. Bake for about 30 minutes, or until just set.

COOK'S TIP When working with fragile pastry like this, try rolling it out over the loose base of the flan tin, ready to lift it up and carefully ease it into the tin surround.

Full-flavoured Alphonso mangoes, which are available in late spring, are best for this dish if you can locate them.

GRIDDLED MANGO with LIME SYRUP SORBET

1 Place the sugar in a heavy pan and add 250ml | 8fl oz | 1 cup water. Heat gently until the sugar has dissolved. Increase the heat and boil for 5 minutes. Cool completely. Add the lime juice and any pulp that has collected in the squeezer. Strain the mixture and reserve 200ml | 7fl oz | scant 1 cup in a bowl with the star anise.

2 Pour the remaining liquid into a measuring jug or cup and make up to 600ml | 1 pint | 2½ cups with cold water. Mix well.

3 **BY HAND:** pour into a freezerproof container. Freeze for 1½ hours, stir well and return to the freezer for another hour until set. Transfer the sorbet mixture to a food processor and pulse to a smooth ice purée. Freeze for another hour or longer, if wished.
USING AN ICE CREAM MAKER: pour the liquid into the bowl and churn until thick. Transfer to a freezerproof container and freeze for at least 30 minutes before serving.

4 Pour the reserved syrup into a pan and boil for 2–3 minutes, or until thickened a little. Leave to cool. Cut the cheeks from either side of the stone (pit) on each unpeeled mango, and score the flesh on each in a diamond pattern. Brush with a little oil. Heat a griddle, until very hot and a few drops of water sprinkled on the surface evaporate instantly. Lower the heat a little and griddle the mango halves, cut side down, for 30–60 seconds until branded with golden griddle marks.

5 Invert the mango cheeks on individual plates and serve hot or cold with the syrup drizzled over and a scoop or two of sorbet. Decorate with the reserved star anise.

INGREDIENTS
serves six

250g | 9oz | 1¼ cups sugar

juice of 6 limes

3 star anise

6 small or 3 medium to large mangoes

groundnut (peanut) oil, for brushing

Exotic fruits are the perfect choice for a refreshing fruit salad, especially when they are flavoured and sweetened with lime and coffee liqueur.

FRAGRANT FRUIT SALAD

INGREDIENTS
serves six

130g | 4¹/₂oz | scant ³/₄ cup sugar

thinly pared rind and juice of 1 lime

60ml | 4 tbsp coffee liqueur, such as Tia Maria, Kahlúa or Toussaint

1 small pineapple

1 papaya

2 pomegranates

1 medium mango

2 passion fruits

fine strips of lime peel, to decorate

1 Put the sugar and lime rind in a small pan with 150ml | ¹/₄ pint | ²/₃ cup water. Heat gently until the sugar dissolves, then bring to the boil and simmer for 5 minutes. Leave to cool, then strain into a large serving bowl. Stir in the lime juice and liqueur.

2 Using a sharp knife, cut the plume and stalk end from the pineapple. Peel thickly and cut the flesh into bitesize pieces, discarding the woody central core. Add to the bowl.

3 Cut the papaya in half and scoop out the seeds. Cut away the skin, then cut into slices. Cut the pomegranates in half and scoop out the seeds. Break into clusters and add to the bowl.

4 Cut the mango lengthways, along each side of the stone (pit). Peel the skin off the flesh. Cut into slices and add with the rest of the fruit to the bowl. Stir well.

5 Halve the passion fruits and scoop out the flesh using a teaspoon. Spoon over the salad and serve, decorated with fine strips of lime peel.

COOK'S TIP To maximize the flavour of the fruit, allow the salad to stand at room temperature for an hour before serving.

Make the most of rhubarb's short season by enjoying this classic combination of rhubarb and ginger in a mouthwatering ice cream made with mascarpone.

RHUBARB and GINGER ICE CREAM

INGREDIENTS
serves four to six

5 pieces of preserved stem ginger

450g | 1lb | trimmed rhubarb, sliced

115g | 4oz | generous ½ cup caster (superfine) sugar

30ml | 2 tbsp water

150g | 5oz | ²/₃ cup mascarpone

150ml | ¼ pint | ²/₃ cup whipping cream

wafer baskets, to serve (optional)

1 Using a sharp knife, roughly chop the stem ginger and set it aside. Put the rhubarb slices into a pan and add the sugar and water. Cover and simmer for 5 minutes, or until the rhubarb is just tender and still bright pink.

2 Tip the mixture into a food processor or blender. Process until smooth, leave to cool and then chill.

3 BY HAND: mix together the mascarpone, cream and ginger with the rhubarb purée.
USING AN ICE CREAM MAKER: churn the rhubarb purée for 15–20 minutes, or until it is thick.

4 BY HAND: pour the mixture into a plastic tub or similar freezerproof container and freeze for 6 hours, or until firm, beating once or twice during the freezing time to break up the ice crystals.
USING AN ICE CREAM MAKER: put the mascarpone into a bowl, soften it with a wooden spoon, then gradually beat in the cream. Add the chopped ginger, then transfer to the ice cream maker and churn until the ice cream is firm.

5 Serve as scoops in bowls or wafer baskets or cups.

COOK'S TIP If the rhubarb purée is rather pale, add a few drops of pink colouring when mixing in the cream.

This refreshing sorbet is perfect for a lazy afternoon in the garden.

MINTED EARL GREY SORBET

1 Put the caster sugar and water into a pan and bring the mixture to the boil, stirring until the sugar has dissolved.

2 Thinly pare the rind from the lemon so that it falls straight into the pan of syrup. Simmer for 2 minutes then pour into a bowl. Cool, and then chill.

3 Put the tea into a pan and pour on the boiling water. Cover and leave to stand for 5 minutes, then strain into a bowl. Cool, and then chill.

4 BY HAND: pour the tea into a plastic tub or similar freezerproof container. Strain in the chilled syrup. Freeze for 4 hours.
USING AN ICE CREAM MAKER: combine the tea and syrup and churn the mixture until thick.

5 BY HAND: lightly whisk the egg white until just frothy. Scoop the sorbet into a food processor, process until smooth and mix in the mint and egg white. Spoon back into the tub and freeze for 4 hours, or until firm.
USING AN ICE CREAM MAKER: add the mint to the mixture. Lightly whisk the egg white until just frothy, then tip it into the ice cream maker and continue to churn until firm enough to scoop.

6 Serve in scoops, decorated with a few fresh or frosted mint leaves.

COOK'S TIP If you have only Earl Grey tea bags these can be used instead, but add enough to make 450ml | 3/4 pint | scant 2 cups strong tea. Make frosted mint leaves to serve by dipping the leaves in egg white and sprinkling them with caster sugar.

INGREDIENTS
serves six

200g | 7oz | 1 cup caster (superfine) sugar

300ml | 1/2 pint | 1 1/4 cups water

1 lemon, well scrubbed

45ml | 3 tbsp Earl Grey tea leaves

450ml | 3/4 pint | scant 2 cups boiling water

1 egg white

30ml | 2 tbsp chopped fresh mint leaves

fresh mint sprigs or frosted mint, to decorate

Summer Cooking

INTRODUCTION

Summer is the season for celebrating the finest fresh ingredients. Wandering through the garden fills the senses with the scents of herbs and the visual beauty of abundant produce. A wealth of fruit and vegetable shapes, colours and textures creates a wonderful display in the warm sunshine.

Events in the garden are mirrored in the marketplace, as supermarkets stack their shelves with local goods as well as fruit and vegetables from distant suppliers, and market stalls fill with a cornucopia of ingredients at affordable prices. In the summer months there is almost unlimited choice and those who are not faced with a home-grown glut of crops have to be strong-willed to resist the temptation to overstock in sheer enthusiasm for the quality of fresh foods available.

Summer style

When the weather is hot the cooking should be easy. This is not the season for spending hours standing over a hot stove – sociable dishes that make the most of quick methods and sunny days are far more fun.

Cooking outdoors on a barbecue provides the ideal opportunity for sharing the work. Everyone takes some responsibility for basting and turning tender cuts and succulent vegetables over hot coals. Whether it is in the back garden or on a beach with friends, there cannot be many better ways to eat when it is warm enough. The smallest helping hands can pass around plates if they are the shatterproof kind.

Picnics are the other perfect answer to summer eating. They can be humble or ostentatious, according to mood and occasion. Even the simplest sandwich becomes irresistible in summertime – sweet, ripe and lightly salted tomatoes are fabulous in lightly buttered, spongy fresh bread.

Today's picnickers are just as likely to pack chilled soups, marinated chargrilled vegetables and tempting savoury flans alongside traditional salads. Grand picnic hampers, which were once heavily laden with pies, cold meat roasts and elaborately garnished terrines, are lightened and enlivened by modern salad fusions of fruit and vegetables with peppery leaves, handfuls of aromatic herbs and bright edible flowers. Meanwhile, glorious cheeses and oil-drizzled charcuterie are exciting and easy alternatives to intimidating pies and rich cream coatings on cold poached poultry.

Informal and fun

In the summer months formal dining can be abandoned completely to a more relaxed approach, even for special celebrations. From lazy weekend parties to summer weddings, the mood is more of soirée than silver service, with the emphasis on pre-planning to share and spread the workload, rather than a huge last-minute effort.

Summer buffets are most likely to be cold, with an eclectic selection of simple finger food or fork dishes for effortless eating. Dinner and supper parties are often centred on a salad-style main dish of hot and cold ingredients, flanked by pasta to start and fresh berries to finish. Leisurely sampling and savouring in airy surroundings replaces regimented courses served in the comforting warmth of a kitchen or dining room.

Everyday meals are light and healthy, with the focus on Mediterranean-style recipes, Asian stir-fries and fresh seafood. Several separate savouries may be eaten individually with warm bread instead of a combination of main dish, its starchy accompaniment and complementary vegetables. Fresh fruit and refreshing sorbets or ice creams are especially welcome desserts – they are also excellent snacks.

Flavours of summer

Summer takes many by surprise. One minute there is a limited harvest of tasty spring vegetables to be selected with care and the next the growing season seems to go mad. From precious quantities of young crops to overflowing basketfuls of vegetables and soft fruit – many gardeners have experienced the strange sensation of cultivating courgettes (zucchini) and pumpkins that seem to grow before their very eyes.

Many spring vegetables continue to provide ample supplies throughout the summer, changing from baby first crop to mature produce. Salad leaves crop continuously and successive plantings ensure a steady harvest rather than sudden gluts. In a good year, huge crops of green beans tax the creativity of most cooks. Tomatoes, strawberries and raspberries are all likely to yield big crops in some years, and successive generations of cooks have mastered favourite methods of preserving summer produce.

SIMPLY FREEZING

Freezing is the easiest and most successful method of preserving large quantities of fresh fruit and vegetables. The most important point is to wash, dry, trim and prepare the fruit or vegetables before freezing, so that they will be ready to cook straight from frozen. Green beans, berries and soft fruit are favourite freezer candidates.

Blanching is largely unnecessary – tests have shown that the difference it makes is negligible over periods of 6–9 months – but adequate packing in thick, well-sealed bags is important to keep the produce in good condition. Open freezing provides "free flow" separated items direct from the freezer. Spread fruit or beans on trays lined with baking parchment and place in the freezer. As soon as they are frozen, place into bags and seal as normal. Then you will be able to remove small amounts without the pieces breaking up. Freezing large batches of soups, purées and sauces is an excellent way of preserving vegetables, like tomatoes, that don't freeze well raw.

DRYING AND SEMI-DRYING

In suitable climates, drying is a brilliant method of concentrating the flavour of vegetables such as peppers and tomatoes. When the luxury of stringing up prepared and cut vegetables to dry in the sun is not available, slowly roasting them to a concentrated semi-dried state in a barely warm oven is a good way of reducing their volume. They should be laid out on a rack and turned occasionally. Once dried and cooled, they can be packed in olive oil in sterilized jars, covered and stored in the refrigerator; alternatively, the concentrated vegetables can be frozen – ideal for adding to salads and pasta.

Drying is the traditional method of preserving herbs for winter use. While it may not be suitable for the soft-leafed varieties, as they will disintegrate, it is still a good method for some of the woody herbs, such as rosemary, sage and thyme. Wash and dry the sprigs, then hang them upside down in a warm, dry place. Enclose each bunch in a brown paper bag, tying it neatly around the stems. When the herbs are thoroughly crisp and dry they can be stored in an airtight jar in a cool, dark place.

SUMMER PRESERVES

• Jams, jellies and syrups are all ideal for soft fruit, especially currants and gooseberries which are rich in pectin and full-flavoured raspberries and strawberries.

• Tomatoes can be used in chutneys and ketchups.

• Flavoured vinegars are excellent made with fruit or herbs, such as raspberries, black-currants, peaches, basil, tarragon or chives. Use good-quality ripe fruit and perfect herbs and macerate for 2–5 days in wine vinegar or cider vinegar, crushing frequently. Strain and sweeten fruit vinegars, then pour into clean sterilized bottles and store in a cool, dark place. Use in dressings, sauces and drinks. Herb vinegars make good salad dressings and sauces, especially flavoured cider vinegar or balsamic vinegar, which can be used for deglazing pan juices after cooking meat or fish.

Cool cooking

Being outdoors is the best way to make the most of summer, so smart cooks cut down on kitchen time without compromising on quality. The following are a few suggestions for achieving the best balance by following the "less is more" principle.

SOURCING THE BEST

Although nothing can better the flavour of ingredients that have come straight from the ground, food that has only been transported for a few hours is the next best thing. Fruit and vegetables that are flown halfway across the world are picked under-ripe to ensure that they still have a shelf life when they reach the supermarket. Although they may look perfect or be a regulation size, their flavour is usually lacklustre. Check the labels on packets, shelving and boxes to find food that is produced as close to home as possible.

RAW GOODNESS

Serve good produce raw as crudités, in salads or in cold uncooked soups (such as gazpacho) and fruit or vegetable juices and smoothies. This not only saves time but also results in dishes that are full of flavour, texture and vitamin goodness.

COOK AHEAD

Cooking early, in the cool of the morning, or late in the evening is a good way of avoiding hot sessions in the heat of day. Braised dishes and light casseroles can be reheated just before serving and baked or boiled ham can be left to cool and served cold. Cool the cooked food as quickly as possible, then chill it until ready to serve.

FRESH IS BEST

- Make the most of your garden, planters and hanging baskets to cultivate as much fresh produce as possible. This way you KNOW it is good.

- Buy from local growers, organic if possible, for the most healthy and flavoursome produce.

- Take advantage of local seafood if you live near the coast or take a cool box if you visit a port where fresh fish and shellfish are landed.

SELECTING FOR SIMPLICITY

- Fish and shellfish are light and they cook quickly.

- Light poultry, such as chicken or duck breast fillets, and tender cuts of meat cook quickly.

- The best cuts and ingredients invariably make the best end results with less fuss.

PRACTICAL PREPARATION

- Keep preparation of fresh fruit and vegetables to a minimum to preserve nutrients and time.

- Balance minimum peeling with fine cutting and slicing, so that ingredients cook quickly.

- Marinating moistens food before grilling (broiling) or cooking on a barbecue and negates need for heavy sauces. Oil, fruit juice and yogurt are all excellent mediums for marinades.

LIGHT METHODS AND SHORT TIMES

- Cook fresh, finely cut produce briefly – stir-frying in the minimum oil or butter.

- Grilling, pan-frying, cooking on a barbecue and roasting for short times at a high temperature are ideal for fine cuts of fish, chicken and meat.

- Light poaching and brief simmering are good methods for fish, chicken, eggs and vegetables.

Success with summer ingredients

Here are six categories of ingredients divided by their type and the cooking and preparation methods used.

1 TENDER-SKINNED PRODUCE

The vegetable-fruits are at their best in summer. Tomatoes, cucumber, courgettes (zucchini), aubergines (eggplant) and (bell) peppers can all do without peeling.

- Select plump, firm and smooth examples that have not been bruised or battered. Wash them well and dry them on a dishtowel.
- Discard the stalk ends and cut out any tough core or stalk from tomatoes.
- Remove the seeds and pith from inside peppers.
- To remove the seeds from cucumber, cut the cucumber in half lengthways and scoop out the seeds with a teaspoon.

2 ROOTS, STEMS AND TUBERS

Remove dirt. They usually have to be trimmed and may need to be peeled, depending on the recipe. Remember that most of the vitamins lie under the skin.

- Scrub root vegetables, such as carrots, potatoes and turnips, if they are not to be peeled before cooking and remove any "eyes" or similar marks.
- Boil beetroot (beet) in its skin. Trim off the leaf, leaving stalk and root ends in place. Slide off the skin from the freshly cooked, hot beetroot.
- Celery and fennel should be thoroughly washed to remove dirt from between the layers of stem. Cut heads of fennel in half and trim the tough core from the fennel.
- Corn can be grilled (broiled) or roasted in its outer husk but the fine silky threads should be removed first and the husk replaced around the kernels. Remove all the covering to boil the corn. To remove the kernels, cut down the outside of the cob with a sharp knife.

3 SHOOTS AND LEAVES

Wash by swirling in cold water. Do not leave them to soak. Separate the leaves and wash their bases well to remove grit and insects. Dry in a salad spinner, or on a clean dishtowel. If you are feeling energetic, swing the towel around outside.

- Leaves may be torn or finely cut according to taste, but they should be prepared as close as possible to serving, otherwise they become sad and limp.
- Beans should be washed and trimmed. Some beans have tough strings running down their sides – use a sharp knife or potato peeler to remove these. Slice beans into lengths, or cut them at a slant into long, fine strips.

4 STONE/PIT FRUIT

Stone fruit should be firm, plump and bright in colour. Hard green fruit is unripe and tasteless – leave on a sunny windowsill until ripe. Stone fruit is excellent raw or poached; larger fruits, such as peaches and nectarines, are succulent grilled (broiled) or baked. They are good in jams, jellies, syrups and vinegars.

- To peel peaches, place them in a bowl and pour in boiling water. Leave to stand for 30–60 seconds, then drain and slit the skin with the point of a knife. The skin will now peel off.

- To stone (pit) peaches, plums and apricots, cut the fruit in half, following the indentation. Hold one half and twist the other, then lift it off the stone. Cut the stone out of the other half.

- A cherry pitter is used to remove the pits from cherries. Place the cherry in the small cup and push the hinged spike through it, driving the pit out through the hollow base.

5 SOFT FRUITS

Look for fruit that has a good colour and is firm and ripe. These are all good raw or lightly cooked. Currants and most gooseberries are very sharp raw and are often poached and sweetened. Currants have a high pectin content and make excellent set preserves; raspberries and mulberries have a medium pectin content; strawberries have a low pectin content but they make a softly set preserve when combined with lemon juice.

- To string currants, hold the stalk in one hand and slide the prongs of a fork down the stalk.

- To hull strawberries, grasp the fruit in one hand and twist out the stalk, pulling away the long hull at the same time.

- Figs have tender skins that can be eaten or peeled away as preferred. Wash and trim off the stalk end, then cut in half or quarters, leaving the sections attached at the base.

6 SCENTS OF SUMMER

Summer is the time to cultivate soft-leafed herbs and edible flowers. French tarragon, chives, basil, flat-leaf or curly parsley, dill, sweet cicely, fennel and chervil are all excellent. Coriander (cilantro) also grows well under glass. If ground space is limited, plant in pots or window boxes, while big hanging baskets look brilliant filled with herbs.

- Preserve fresh herbs by freezing. Wash and dry the herbs, then place tender sprigs in freezer bags. It is well worth growing large batches, then freezing them for winter use.

- Basil, coriander, mint, chives, rocket (arugula) and fennel are all excellent for making pesto-style pastes. Grind the washed herbs with pine kernels and garlic, adding plenty of olive oil to make a thin paste, then store in sterilized airtight jars in the refrigerator.

- Make full use of edible flowers such as chives, thyme, courgette (zucchini) flowers, violets, nasturtiums, chrysanthemums, elderflower, lavender and rose petals. Adding them to salads brings a vivid sense of summer to the table. They can also be used in more adventurous ways, for example, in fritters, to flavour ices, drinks and sauces, and to flavour sugar.

Ripe and Juicy

Crisp green beans, peppers and temptingly juicy
tomatoes are all in glut at this time of year.
Use them in chilled soups and tasty appetizers.
Fresh corn is delicious spiced up with chillies,
or, as a treat for the kids, cooked on the barbecue
smothered in plenty of butter.

A piquant and fresh-tasting chilled soup from the kitchens of Spain, gazpacho is as popular today as it was when first made many centuries ago.

CLASSIC GAZPACHO

INGREDIENTS
serves six

900g | 2lb ripe tomatoes, peeled, and seeded if you like

1 cucumber, peeled and roughly chopped

2 red (bell) peppers, seeded and roughly chopped

2 garlic cloves, crushed

1 large onion, roughly chopped

30ml | 2 tbsp white wine vinegar

120ml | 4fl oz | 1/2 cup olive oil

250g | 9oz | 4 1/2 cups fresh white breadcrumbs

450ml | 3/4 pint | scant 2 cups iced water

salt and freshly ground black pepper

ice cubes, to serve

for the garnish

30–45ml | 2–3 tbsp olive oil

4 thick slices bread, cut into small cubes

2 tomatoes, peeled and finely diced

1 small onion, very finely sliced

fresh flat leaf parsley, chopped

1 In a large bowl, mix the tomatoes, cucumber, peppers, garlic and onion. Stir in the vinegar, oil, breadcrumbs and water until well mixed. Purée the mixture in a food processor or blender until almost smooth and pour into a large bowl. If the soup is too thick, add a little cold water. Add salt and pepper to taste and chill.

2 To make the garnish, heat the oil in a frying pan and add the bread cubes.

3 Cook over a medium heat for 5–6 minutes, stirring occasionally to brown evenly. Drain on kitchen paper and put into a small bowl. Place the remaining garnishing ingredients into separate bowls or on to a serving plate.

4 Ladle the gazpacho into bowls and add ice cubes to each, then serve immediately. Pass around the bowls of garnishing ingredients with the soup so that they can be added to taste.

VARIATIONS If any of your guests find raw onion difficult to digest, you can leave it out. Alternatively, spice up with an extra clove of garlic and a dash of chilli sauce.

A coolly elegant dish for an *al fresco* dinner party. Use different melons to create a subtle contrast in flavour and colour. Try a combination of Charentais and Ogen or cantaloupe melon.

MELON SOUP with MINT and MELON SORBET

INGREDIENTS
serves six to eight

2.25kg | 5–5¼lb very ripe melon

45ml | 3 tbsp orange juice

30ml | 2 tbsp lemon juice

mint leaves, to garnish

for the mint and melon sorbet

25g | 1oz | 2 tbsp granulated sugar

120ml | 4fl oz | ½ cup water

2.25kg | 5–5¼lb very ripe melon

juice of 2 limes

30ml | 2 tbsp chopped fresh mint

1 To make the mint and melon sorbet (sherbet), put the sugar and water into a pan and heat gently until the sugar dissolves. Bring to the boil and simmer for 4–5 minutes, then remove from the heat and leave to cool.

2 Halve the melon. Scrape out the seeds, then cut it into large wedges and cut the flesh out of the skin. Weigh about 1.5kg | 3–3½lb melon.

3 Purée the melon in a food processor or blender with the cooled syrup and lime juice.

4 Stir in the mint and pour the melon mixture into an ice cream maker. Churn, following the manufacturer's instructions, or until the sorbet is smooth and firm. Alternatively, pour the mixture into a suitable container and freeze until icy around the edges. Transfer to a food processor or blender and process until smooth. Repeat the freezing and processing two or three times or until smooth and holding its shape, then freeze until firm.

5 To make the chilled melon soup, prepare the melon as in step 2 and purée it in a food processor or blender. Pour the purée into a bowl and stir in the orange and lemon juice. Place the soup in the refrigerator for 30–40 minutes, but do not chill it for too long as this will dull its flavour.

6 Ladle the soup into bowls and add a large scoop of the sorbet to each. Garnish with mint leaves and serve immediately.

This luxurious Middle Eastern dip is perfect for a picnic. The quantities can be varied according to taste, depending on how creamy or tart you want it to be.

BABA GHANOUSH

1 Place the aubergines directly over the flame of a gas stove or on the coals of a barbecue. Turn the aubergines fairly frequently until deflated and the skin is evenly charred. Remove from the heat with a pair of tongs.

2 Put the aubergines in a plastic bag or in a bowl and seal tightly. Leave to cool for 30–60 minutes.

3 Peel off the blackened skin from the aubergines, reserving the juices. Chop the aubergine flesh, either by hand for a textured result or in a food processor for a smooth purée. Put the aubergine in a bowl and stir in the reserved juices.

4 Add the garlic and tahini to the aubergine and stir until smooth and well combined. Stir in the lemon juice, which will thicken the mixture. If the mixture becomes too thick, add 15–30ml | 1–2 tbsp water or more lemon juice, if you like. Season with cumin and salt to taste.

5 Spoon the mixture into a serving bowl. Drizzle with olive oil and garnish with fresh coriander leaves, hot pepper sauce and olives and | or pickled cucumbers and peppers. Serve at room temperature with pitta bread or chunks of crusty French bread.

INGREDIENTS
serves two to four

1 large or 2 medium aubergines (eggplant)

2–4 garlic cloves, chopped, to taste

90–150ml | 6–10 tbsp tahini

juice of 1 lemon, or to taste

1.5ml | 1/4 tsp ground cumin, or to taste

salt

extra virgin olive oil, for drizzling

fresh coriander (cilantro) leaves, hot pepper sauce and a few olives and | or pickled cucumbers and (bell) peppers

pitta bread or chunks of crusty French bread, to serve

Keeping the husk on the corn protects the kernels and encloses the butter, so the flavours are contained. Fresh corn with husks intact is perfect, but banana leaves or a double layer of foil are also suitable.

HUSK-GRILLED CORN on the COB

1 Heat a heavy frying pan. Add the dried chillies and roast them by stirring them continuously for 1 minute without letting them scorch. Put them in a bowl with almost boiling water to cover. Use a saucer to keep them submerged, and leave them to rehydrate for up to 1 hour. Drain, remove the seeds and chop the chillies finely.

2 Place the butter in a bowl and add the chillies, lemon juice and parsley. Season to taste and mix well.

3 Peel back the husks from each cob without tearing them. Remove the silk. Smear about 30ml|2 tbsp of the chilli butter over each cob. Pull the husks back over the cobs, ensuring that the butter is well hidden. Put the rest of the butter in a pot, smooth the top and chill to use later. Place the cobs in a bowl of cold water and leave in a cool place for 1–3 hours; longer if that suits your work plan better.

4 Prepare the barbecue, if using, or heat the grill (broiler) to its highest setting. Remove the corn cobs from the water and wrap in pairs in foil. Once the flames have died down, position a lightly oiled grill rack over the coals to heat. When the coals are medium-hot, or have a moderate coating of ash, cook the corn for 15–20 minutes. Remove the foil and cook them for about 5 minutes more, turning them often to char the husks a little. Serve hot, with the rest of the butter.

INGREDIENTS
serves six

3 dried chipotle chillies

250g | 9oz | generous 1 cup butter, softened

7.5ml | 1 1/2 tsp lemon juice

45ml | 3 tbsp chopped fresh flat leaf parsley

6 corn on the cob, with husks intact

salt and ground black pepper

The sweet aniseed flavours of sweet cicely and fennel combine beautifully with the succulent tastes of the peppers and tomatoes and piquant capers. Sweet cicely leaves make an excellent garnish and they taste just like the flowers. This dish can be served as a light lunch in hot weather or as an unusual first course for a dinner party.

ROASTED PEPPERS with SWEET CICELY

INGREDIENTS
serves four

4 red (bell) peppers, halved and deseeded

8 small or 4 medium tomatoes

15ml | 1 tbsp semi-ripe sweet cicely seeds

15ml | 1 tbsp fennel seeds

15ml | 1 tbsp capers

8 sweet cicely flowers, newly opened, stems removed

60ml | 4 tbsp olive oil

crusty bread, to serve

for the garnish

a few small sweet cicely leaves

8 more flowers, heads left intact on the stems

1 Preheat the oven to 180°C/350°F/Gas 4. Place the red pepper halves in a large ovenproof dish and set aside.

2 To skin the tomatoes, cut a cross at the base, then pour over boiling water and leave them to stand for 30 seconds to 1 minute. Cut them in half if they are of medium size.

3 Place a whole small or half a medium tomato in each half of a pepper cavity.

4 Cover with a scattering of semi-ripe sweet cicely seeds, fennel seeds and capers and about half the sweet cicely flowers. Drizzle the olive oil all over.

5 Bake in the top of the oven for 1 hour. Remove from the oven and add the rest of the flowers. Garnish with fresh sweet cicely leaves and flowers and serve with lots of crusty bread to soak up the juices.

COOK'S TIP Try adding the stems from the sweet cicely to the water in which fruit is stewed. They will add a delightful flavour and reduce the need for sugar.

VARIATIONS If sweet cicely is not available, this dish can also be made with a range of different herbs, although they will all impart a distinctive flavour. Celery leaves, chervil and lovage are some you might like to try.

This is a real summer favourite, using the best ripe plum tomatoes and tenderest green beans.

GREEN BEANS with TOMATOES

1 Heat the oil in a large frying pan. Add the onion and garlic and cook for about 5 minutes, until the onion is softened but not brown.

2 Add the chopped tomatoes, white wine, beans, olives and lemon juice and cook over a low heat for 20 more minutes, stirring occasionally, until the sauce is thickened and the beans are tender. Season with salt and pepper to taste and serve immediately.

COOK'S TIP Green beans need little preparation and now that they are grown without the string, you simply trim the ends. When choosing, make sure that the beans snap easily – this is a good sign of freshness.

INGREDIENTS
serves four

30ml | 2 tbsp olive oil

1 large onion, finely sliced

2 garlic cloves, finely chopped

6 large ripe plum tomatoes, peeled, seeded and coarsely chopped

150ml | 1/4 pint | 2/3 cup dry white wine

450g | 1lb runner (green) beans, sliced in half lengthways

16 pitted black olives

30ml | 2 tbsp lemon juice

salt and freshly ground black pepper

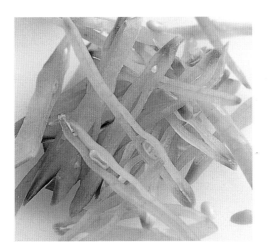

Delicate and Aromatic

This chapter makes full use of the many herbs available at
this time of year – for salads and light main courses to be
eaten *al fresco* with fresh vegetables. Chives and savory,
fennel, basil, parsley, oregano and dill are all used, but
most can be replaced by those you have in abundance.

This combination is inspired by the Turkish tradition of eating sweet, juicy watermelon with salty white cheese in the hot summer months.

SALAD with WATERMELON and FETA CHEESE

INGREDIENTS
serves four

30–45ml | 2–3 tbsp extra virgin olive oil

juice of 1/2 lemon

5ml | 1 tsp vinegar of choice or to taste

sprinkling of fresh thyme leaves

pinch of ground cumin

4 large slices of watermelon, chilled

1 frisée lettuce, core removed

130g | 41/2oz feta cheese, preferably sheep's milk feta, cut into bitesize pieces

handful of lightly toasted pumpkin seeds

handful of sunflower seeds

10–15 black olives

1 Pour the extra virgin olive oil, lemon juice and vinegar into a bowl or jug (pitcher). Add the fresh thyme and ground cumin and whisk until well combined. Set the dressing aside until you are ready to serve the salad.

2 Cut the rind off the watermelon and remove as many seeds as possible. Cut the flesh into triangular shaped chunks.

3 Put the lettuce leaves in a bowl, pour over the dressing and toss together. Arrange the leaves on a serving dish or individual plates and add the watermelon, feta cheese, pumpkin and sunflower seeds and black olives. Serve the salad immediately.

COOK'S TIP The best choice of olives for this recipe are plump black Mediterranean olives such as kalamata, other shiny, brined varieties or dry-cured black olives such as the Italian ones.

This is an Israeli dish of fresh summer vegetables and fragrant dill tossed in a rich sour cream sauce.

SUMMER SQUASH and BABY NEW POTATOES

1 Cut the squash into pieces about the same size as the potatoes. Put the potatoes in a pan and add water to cover, with the sugar and salt. Bring to the boil, then simmer for about 10 minutes – until almost tender. Add the squash and continue to cook until the vegetables are just tender, then drain.

2 Melt the butter in a large pan. Fry the spring onions until just wilted, then gently stir in the dill and vegetables.

3 Remove the pan from the heat and stir in the sour cream or yogurt. Return to the heat and stir gently until warm. Season with salt and pepper and serve.

COOK'S TIP Choose small specimens of squash with bright skins that are free from blemishes and bruises.

INGREDIENTS
serves four

400g | 14oz mixed squash, such as yellow and green courgettes (zucchini) and pale green or yellow patty pans

400g | 14oz baby new potatoes

pinch of sugar

40-75g | 1¹/₂-3oz | 3-6 tbsp butter

2 bunches spring onions (scallions), thinly sliced

1 large bunch fresh dill, finely chopped

300ml | ¹/₂ pint | 1¹/₄ cups sour cream or Greek (US strained plain) yogurt

salt and freshly ground black pepper

This is so typically Italian that if you close your eyes you could be on a Tuscan hillside, sitting under a shady tree and enjoying an elegant lunch. Fennel has many fans, but is often used only in its raw state or lightly braised, making this griddle recipe a delightful discovery.

GRIDDLED FENNEL SALAD with OLIVES

INGREDIENTS
serves six

3 sweet baby orange (bell) peppers

5 fennel bulbs with green tops, total weight about 900g | 2lb

30ml | 2 tbsp olive oil

15ml | 1 tbsp cider vinegar or white wine vinegar

45ml | 3 tbsp extra virgin olive oil

24 small Niçoise olives

2 fresh savory sprigs, leaves removed

salt and ground black pepper

1 Heat a griddle until a few drops of water sprinkled on to the surface evaporate instantly. Roast the baby peppers, turning them every few minutes until charred all over. Remove the pan from the heat, place the peppers in a bowl and cover with clear film (plastic wrap).

2 Remove the green fronds from the fennel and reserve. Slice the fennel lengthways into five roughly equal pieces. If the root looks a little tough, cut it out. Place the fennel pieces in a flat dish, coat with the olive oil and season. Rub off the charred skin from the grilled peppers, remove the seeds and cut the flesh into small dice.

3 Re-heat the griddle and test the temperature again, then lower the heat slightly and grill the fennel slices in batches for about 8–10 minutes, turning frequently, until they are branded with golden grill marks. Monitor the heat so they cook through without over-charring. As each batch cooks, transfer it to a flat serving dish.

4 Whisk the vinegar and extra virgin olive oil together, then pour the dressing over the fennel. Gently fold in the diced baby orange peppers and the olives. Tear the savory leaves and fennel fronds and scatter them over the salad. Serve warm or cold.

COOK'S TIP If cooking directly on the barbecue, char the peppers when the coals are hot, then cool them ready for peeling. Cook the fennel over medium hot coals and turn frequently once stripes have formed.

This crunchy salad bursting with the flavours of fresh herbs makes an ideal light lunch or supper. Serve it with crème fraîche or yogurt cheese.

WILD GREENS and OLIVES

INGREDIENTS
serves four

1 large bunch wild rocket (arugula), about 115g | 4oz

1 large bunch mixed salad leaves

1/4 white cabbage, thinly sliced

1 cucumber, sliced

1 small red onion, chopped

2–3 garlic cloves, chopped

3–5 tomatoes, cut into wedges

1 green (bell) pepper, seeded and sliced

2–3 fresh mint sprigs, sliced or torn

15–30ml | 1–2 tbsp chopped fresh parsley and | or tarragon or dill

pinch of dried oregano or thyme

45ml | 3 tbsp extra virgin olive oil

juice of 1/2 lemon

15ml | 1 tbsp red wine vinegar

15–20 black olives

salt and freshly ground black pepper

crème fraîche or yogurt cheese, to serve

1 In a large salad bowl, put the rocket, mixed salad leaves, white cabbage, cucumber, onion and garlic. Toss gently with your fingers to combine the leaves and vegetables.

2 Arrange the tomatoes, pepper and fresh herbs on top of the greens and vegetables. Sprinkle over the dried oregano or thyme and season. Drizzle over the oil, lemon juice and vinegar, stud with the olives and serve.

COOK'S TIPS Try to find mixed salad leaves that include varieties such as lamb's lettuce, purslane and mizuna. To make yogurt cheese, mash a little feta into natural (plain) yogurt.

VARIATION Alternatively serve with cottage or cream cheese flavoured with black pepper and herbs.

Here is a risotto to celebrate the abundance of summer herbs. An aromatic blend of oregano, chives, parsley and basil combines with arborio rice to make a creamy and satisfying meal.

FRESH HERB RISOTTO

1 Cook the wild rice in boiling salted water according to the instructions on the packet, then drain and set aside.

2 Heat the butter and oil in a large, heavy pan. When the butter has melted, add the onion and cook for 3 minutes. Add the arborio rice and cook for 2 minutes, stirring to coat.

3 Pour in the dry white wine and bring to the boil. Reduce the heat and cook for 10 minutes, or until all the wine has been absorbed.

4 Add the hot vegetable stock, a little at a time, waiting for each quantity to be absorbed before adding more, and stirring continuously. After 20–25 minutes the rice should be tender and creamy. Season well.

5 Add the herbs and wild rice; heat for 2 minutes, stirring frequently. Stir in two-thirds of the Parmesan and cook until melted. Serve sprinkled with the remaining Parmesan.

COOK'S TIPS Risotto rice is essential to achieve the correct creamy texture in this dish. Other types of rice simply will not do. Fresh herbs are also a must, but you can use tarragon, chervil, marjoram or thyme instead of the ones listed here, if you prefer.

INGREDIENTS
serves four

90g | 3¹/₂oz | ¹/₂ cup wild rice

15ml | 1 tbsp butter

15ml | 1 tbsp olive oil

1 small onion, finely chopped

450g | 1lb | 2¹/₄ cups arborio rice

300ml | ¹/₂ pint | 1¹/₄ cups dry white wine

1.2 litres | 2 pints | 5 cups simmering vegetable stock

45ml | 3 tbsp chopped fresh oregano

45ml | 3 tbsp chopped fresh chives

60ml | 4 tbsp chopped fresh flat leaf parsley

60ml | 4 tbsp chopped fresh basil

75g | 3oz | 1 cup freshly grated Parmesan cheese

salt and freshly ground black pepper

This is a good first course or accompaniment, especially useful for gardeners with a glut of courgettes. You need the large ones that measure about 19cm|7¹/₂in. A barbecue with an adjustable grill is ideal for this recipe, as the wraps need to be seared quickly at the end.

WRAPS with SPINACH and MOZZARELLA

1 Prepare the barbecue or preheat the grill (broiler). To make the dressing, place the garlic in a small pan with water to cover. Bring to the boil, lower the heat and simmer for 5 minutes. Drain. When cool enough to handle, pop the garlic cloves out of their skins and crush to a smooth paste with a little salt. Scrape into a bowl and add the vinegar. Whisk in the oils and season to taste.

2 Slice each courgette lengthways into six or more broad strips, about 3mm|¹/₈in thick. Lay them on a tray. Set aside 5ml|1 tsp of the oil and brush the rest over the courgette strips, evenly coating them with the oil.

3 Place a wok over a high heat. When it starts to smoke, add the reserved oil and stir-fry the spinach for 30 seconds, or until just wilted. Put into a sieve and drain well, then pat the leaves dry with kitchen paper. Tear or slice the mozzarella balls in half and place on kitchen paper to drain.

4 Lay the courgettes on a heated, lightly oiled rack. Cook on one side only for 2–3 minutes, or until striped golden. As each strip cooks, return it to the tray, cooked side up.

5 Place small heaps of spinach towards one end of each courgette strip. Lay two pieces of mozzarella on each pile of spinach. Season well. Use a metal spatula to transfer back to the barbecue rack and cook for about 2 minutes, or until the underside of each has golden-brown stripes. When the cheese starts to melt, fold the courgette over the filling to make a wrap. Lift off carefully and drain on kitchen paper. Serve with the garnish of salad leaves and, if wished, drizzle the dressing over the top.

INGREDIENTS
serves six

2 large yellow courgettes (zucchini), total weight about 675g|1¹/₂lb

45ml|3 tbsp olive oil

250g|9oz baby leaf spinach

250g|9oz mini mozzarella balls

salad burnet, rocket (arugula) and mizuna leaves, to garnish (optional)

salt and ground black pepper

for the dressing

2 whole, unpeeled garlic cloves

30ml|2 tbsp white wine vinegar

30ml|2 tbsp olive oil

15ml|1 tbsp extra virgin olive oil

45ml|3 tbsp walnut oil

This is a light cornmeal pizza base that makes a change from the usual heavy dough. Being wheat-free it is a good recipe for anyone on a restricted diet, while also tasty enough for general consumption.

GRILLED VEGETABLE PIZZA

INGREDIENTS
serves six

1 courgette (zucchini), sliced

1 small or 2 baby aubergines (eggplant), sliced

30ml | 2 tbsp olive oil

1 yellow (bell) pepper, seeded and thickly sliced

115g | 4oz | 1 cup cornmeal

50g | 2oz | ½ cup potato flour

50g | 2oz | ½ cup soya flour

5ml | 1 tsp baking powder

2.5ml | ½ tsp salt

50g | 2oz | ¼ cup soft margarine

about 105ml | 7 tbsp semi-skimmed (low-fat) milk

4 plum tomatoes, skinned and chopped

30ml | 2 tbsp chopped fresh basil

115g | 4oz mozzarella cheese, sliced

salt and ground black pepper

fresh basil leaves, to garnish

1 Preheat the grill (broiler). Brush the courgette and aubergine slices with a little oil and place on a grill rack with the pepper slices. Cook under the grill until lightly browned, turning once.

2 Meanwhile, preheat the oven to 200°C | 400°F | Gas 6. Place the cornmeal, potato flour, soya flour, baking powder and salt in a mixing bowl and stir to mix. Lightly rub in the margarine until the mixture resembles coarse breadcrumbs, then stir in enough milk to make a soft but not sticky dough.

3 Place the dough on a sheet of baking parchment on a baking sheet and roll or press it out to form a 25cm | 10in round, making the edges slightly thicker than the centre.

4 Brush the pizza dough with any remaining oil, then spread the chopped tomatoes over the dough. Sprinkle with the chopped fresh basil and season with salt and pepper. Arrange the grilled vegetables over the tomatoes and top with the cheese.

5 Bake in the oven for 25–30 minutes until crisp and golden brown. Garnish the pizza with fresh basil leaves and serve immediately, cut into slices.

Infused with aromatic herbs and simple to make, this delicate flan makes a delightful lunch dish on a hot day and would be a welcome offering at a picnic.

SUMMER HERB RICOTTA FLAN

1 Preheat the oven to 180°C | 350°F | Gas 4 and lightly grease a 23cm | 9in springform cake tin (pan) with oil. Mix together the ricotta, Parmesan and egg yolks in a food processor or blender. Add the herbs and salt, and blend until smooth and creamy.

2 Whisk the egg whites in a large bowl until they form soft peaks. Gently fold the egg whites into the ricotta mixture, taking care not to knock out too much air. Spoon the ricotta mixture into the tin and smooth the top.

3 Bake for 1 hour 20 minutes or until the flan is risen and the top is golden. Remove from the oven and brush lightly with olive oil, then sprinkle with paprika. Leave the flan to cool before removing from the tin.

4 Make the tapenade. Place the olives and garlic in a food processor or blender and process until finely chopped. Gradually add the olive oil and blend to a coarse paste, then transfer to a serving bowl. Garnish the flan with fresh herb leaves and the reserved olives if wished, and serve with the tapenade.

INGREDIENTS
serves four

olive oil, for greasing and glazing

800g | 1lb 11oz | 3½ cups ricotta cheese

75g | 3oz | 1 cup finely grated Parmesan cheese

3 eggs, separated

60ml | 4 tbsp torn fresh basil leaves

60ml | 4 tbsp chopped fresh chives

45ml | 3 tbsp fresh oregano leaves

2.5ml | ½ tsp salt

2.5ml | ½ tsp paprika

freshly ground black pepper

fresh herb leaves, to garnish

for the tapenade

400g | 14oz | 3½ cups pitted black olives, rinsed and halved, reserving a few whole to garnish (optional)

5 garlic cloves, crushed

75ml | 5 tbsp | ⅓ cup olive oil

This tasty vegetarian main course is easy to make and can be prepared with any number of seasonal vegetables such as spinach, peas, green beans or corn.

SPICED VEGETABLE COUSCOUS

INGREDIENTS
serves six

45ml | 3 tbsp olive oil

1 large onion, finely chopped

2 garlic cloves, crushed

15ml | 1 tbsp tomato purée (paste)

2.5ml | ½ tsp ground turmeric

2.5ml | ½ tsp cayenne pepper

5ml | 1 tsp ground coriander

5ml | 1 tsp ground cumin

225g | 8oz | 1½ cups cauliflower florets

225g | 8oz baby carrots, trimmed

1 red (bell) pepper, seeded and diced

225g | 8oz courgettes (zucchini), sliced

400g | 14oz can chickpeas, drained

4 beefsteak tomatoes, skinned and sliced

45ml | 3 tbsp chopped fresh coriander (cilantro)

450g | 1lb | 2⅔ cups couscous

50g | 2oz | ¼ cup butter or 50ml | 3½ tbsp sunflower oil

salt and ground black pepper

1 Heat 30ml | 2 tbsp of the olive oil in a large pan, add the onion and garlic and cook gently until soft and translucent. Stir in the tomato purée, turmeric, cayenne, coriander and cumin. Cook, stirring, for 2 minutes.

2 Add the cauliflower, baby carrots and pepper, with enough water to come halfway up the vegetables. Bring to the boil, then lower the heat, cover and simmer for 10 minutes.

3 Add the courgettes, chickpeas and tomatoes to the pan and cook for 10 minutes. Stir in the fresh coriander and season. Keep hot.

4 To cook the couscous, bring about 475ml | 16fl oz | 2 cups water to the boil in a large pan. Add the remaining olive oil and 2.5ml | ½ tsp salt. Remove from the heat and add the couscous, stirring. Allow to swell for 2 minutes.

5 Add the butter or sunflower oil, and heat the couscous through gently, stirring to separate the grains.

6 Turn the couscous out on to a warm serving dish, and spoon the cooked vegetables on top, pouring over any liquid. Garnish with sprigs of coriander and serve immediately.

Spicy and Succulent

The last thing you need on a summer's day is to be trapped in the kitchen. Here are some quick recipes to delight family and friends, impressing without exhausting the host. Even the roast chicken could be cooked in the evening and chilled for the next day.

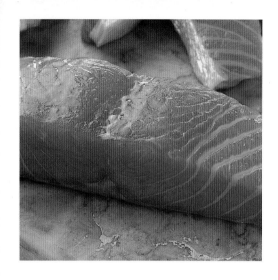

The aroma that wafts out of these fish parcels as you open them is deliciously tempting. If you don't like Eastern flavours, use white wine, herbs and thinly sliced vegetables, or Mediterranean ingredients such as tomatoes, basil and olives.

SALMON in a PARCEL

INGREDIENTS
serves four

2 carrots

2 courgettes (zucchini)

6 spring onions (scallions)

2.5cm | 1in piece of fresh root ginger, peeled

1 lime

2 garlic cloves, thinly sliced

30ml | 2 tbsp teriyaki marinade or Thai fish sauce

5–10ml | 1–2 tsp clear sesame oil

4 salmon fillets, about 200g | 7oz each

ground black pepper

rice, to serve

1 Cut the carrots, courgettes and spring onions into matchsticks and set them aside. Cut the ginger into matchsticks and put these in a small bowl. Using a zester, pare the lime thinly. Add the pared rind to the ginger, with the garlic.

2 Place the teriyaki marinade or Thai fish sauce into a bowl and stir in the juice from the lime and the sesame oil.

3 Preheat the oven to 220°C/425°F/Gas 7. Cut out four rounds of baking parchment, each with a diameter of 40cm/16in. Season the salmon with pepper. Lay a fillet on each paper round, about 3cm/1¹/₄in off centre. Scatter one-quarter of the ginger mixture over each and pile one-quarter of the vegetable matchsticks on top. Spoon one-quarter of the teriyaki or Thai fish sauce mixture over the top.

4 Fold the baking parchment over the salmon and roll the edges of the parchment over to seal each parcel very tightly.

5 Place the salmon parcels on a baking sheet and cook in the oven for 10–12 minutes, depending on the thickness of the fillets. Put the parcels on plates and serve with rice.

VARIATIONS Thick fillets of hake, halibut, hoki and fresh or undyed smoked haddock and cod can all be used for this dish.

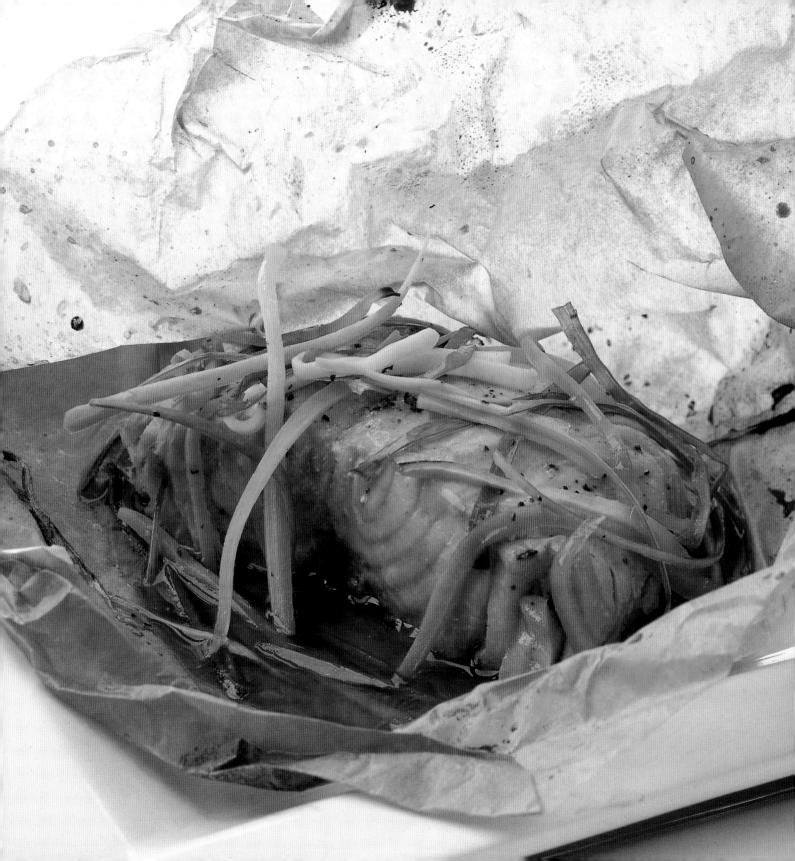

Sardines spiced with cumin and coriander are popular in the coastal regions of Morocco, both in restaurants and as street food. Served with the luscious salad, the only other essential ingredient is fresh crusty bread to mop up the tasty juices.

SPICED SARDINES with FENNEL SALAD

1 Rinse the sardines and pat them dry on kitchen paper, then rub inside and out with a little coarse salt.

2 Dry-roast the cumin and coriander seeds in a small frying pan until they give off their aroma, then grind them using a mortar and pestle or spice grinder.

3 In a bowl, mix the grated onion with the olive oil, cinnamon, ground roasted cumin and coriander, paprika and black pepper. Make several slashes into the flesh of the sardines and smear the onion and spice mixture all over the fish, inside and out and into the gashes. Leave the sardines to stand for about 1 hour to allow the flavours of the spices to penetrate the flesh.

4 Meanwhile, prepare the salad. Peel the grapefruits with a knife, removing all the pith, then peel off the membrane in neat strips down the outside of the fruit. Cut between the membranes to remove the segments of fruit intact. Cut each grapefruit segment in half, place in a bowl and sprinkle with salt.

5 Trim the fennel, cut in half lengthways and slice finely. Add the fennel to the grapefruit with the spring onions, cumin and olive oil. Toss lightly, then garnish with the olives.

6 Preheat the grill (broiler) or barbecue. Cook the sardines for 3–4 minutes on each side, basting with any leftover marinade. Sprinkle with fresh coriander and serve with lemon wedges for squeezing over and the refreshing grapefruit and fennel salad.

INGREDIENTS
serves four to six

12 fresh sardines, gutted

5ml/1 tsp cumin seeds

5ml/1 tsp coriander seeds

1 onion, grated

60–90ml | 4–6 tbsp olive oil

5ml | 1 tsp ground cinnamon

5ml | 1 tsp paprika

5ml | 1 tsp ground black pepper

coarse salt

2 lemons, cut into wedges, and chopped fresh coriander (cilantro), to serve

for the salad

2 ruby grapefruits

5ml | 1 tsp sea salt

1 fennel bulb

2–3 spring onions (scallions), finely sliced

2.5ml | $\frac{1}{2}$ tsp ground roasted cumin

30–45ml | 2–3 tbsp olive oil

handful of black olives, to garnish

Monkfish has a matchless flavour and benefits from being cooked simply. Teaming it with wilted baby spinach and toasted pine nuts is inspirational.

WARM MONKFISH SALAD

INGREDIENTS
serves four

2 monkfish fillets, about 350g | 12oz each

25g | 1oz | 1/4 cup pine nuts

15ml | 1 tbsp olive oil

15g | 1/2oz | 1 tbsp butter

225g | 8oz baby spinach leaves, washed and stalks removed

salt and freshly ground black pepper

for the dressing

5ml | 1 tsp Dijon mustard

5ml | 1 tsp sherry vinegar

60ml | 4 tbsp olive oil

1 garlic clove, crushed

1 Holding the knife at a slight angle, cut each monkfish fillet into 12 diagonal slices. Season lightly and set aside.

2 Heat a frying pan, put in the pine nuts and shake them about for a while until golden brown. Do not allow to burn. Transfer to a plate and set aside.

3 Make the dressing by whisking all the ingredients together until smooth and creamy. Pour the dressing into a small pan, season to taste and heat gently.

4 Heat the oil and butter in a ridged griddle or frying pan until sizzling. Add the fish and sauté for 20–30 seconds on each side.

5 Put the spinach leaves in a large bowl and pour over the warm dressing. Sprinkle on the toasted pine nuts, reserving a few, and toss together well. Divide the dressed spinach leaves among four serving plates and arrange the monkfish slices on top. Scatter the reserved pine nuts on top and serve.

VARIATION Substitute any seasonal salad leaves for the spinach, such as rocket (arugula) or mizuna.

You can vary the seafood in this Italian salad according to what is available, but try to include at least two kinds of shellfish and some squid. The salad is good warm or cold, excellent for a summer dinner party.

SEAFOOD SALAD

1 Put the mussels and clams in a large pan with the white wine. Cover and cook over a high heat, shaking the pan occasionally, for about 4 minutes, until they have opened. Discard any that remain closed. Use a slotted spoon to transfer the shellfish to a bowl, then strain and reserve the cooking liquid and set it aside.

2 Cut the squid into thin rings and chop the tentacles. Leave small squid whole. Halve the scallops horizontally.

3 Heat the oil in a frying pan and add the garlic, chilli, squid, scallops and corals. Sauté for about 2 minutes, until just cooked and tender. Lift the squid and scallops out of the pan and reserve the oil.

4 When the shellfish are cool enough to handle, shell them, keeping a dozen of each in the shell. Peel all but 6–8 of the prawns. Pour the shellfish cooking liquid into a small pan, set over a high heat and reduce by half. Mix all the shelled and unshelled mussels and clams with the squid and scallops, then add the prawns.

5 To make the dressing, whisk the mustard with the vinegar and lemon juice and season to taste. Add the olive oil, whisk vigorously, then whisk in the reserved shellfish cooking liquid and the oil from the frying pan. Pour the dressing over the seafood mixture and toss lightly to coat well.

6 Arrange the chicory and radicchio leaves around the edge of a large serving dish and pile the mixed seafood salad in the centre. Sprinkle with the chopped flat leaf parsley and serve immediately, or chill first.

INGREDIENTS
serves four to six

450g | 1lb live mussels, scrubbed and bearded

450g | 1lb small clams, scrubbed

105ml | 7 tbsp dry white wine

225g | 8oz squid, cleaned

4 large scallops, with their corals

30ml | 2 tbsp olive oil

2 garlic cloves, finely chopped

1 small dried red chilli, crushed

225g | 8oz cooked prawns (shrimp), in the shell

6–8 large chicory (Belgian endive) leaves

6–8 radicchio leaves

15ml | 1 tbsp chopped flat leaf parsley, to garnish

for the dressing

5ml | 1 tsp Dijon mustard

30ml | 2 tbsp white wine vinegar or cider vinegar

5ml | 1 tsp lemon juice

120ml | 4fl oz | 1/2 cup extra virgin olive oil

Even in the summer it is great to enjoy a roast. Rubbing the outside of the bird with lemon, smearing it generously with butter and sprinkling it with salt gives a beautiful deep brown, crisp skin, and keeps the flesh moist and succulent. The garlic roasts to a nutty, melting softness. Eat hot, or chill for a picnic treat.

ROAST CHICKEN with ROASTED GARLIC

INGREDIENTS
serves four

1.6kg | 3¹/₂lb free-range (farm-fresh) chicken

1 lemon

2 bay leaves

1 small bunch fresh thyme

50g | 2oz | ¹/₄ cup butter

4–6 garlic heads

salt and freshly ground black pepper

1 Preheat the oven to 200°C | 400°F | Gas 6. Untie any trussing and tuck the wings under the chicken. Remove any fat from the cavity. Cut the lemon in half and rub all over the chicken. Tuck the lemon inside the cavity with the bay leaves and thyme. Spread the butter all over the breast and legs, seasoning well. Put the bird in a roasting pan.

2 Now prepare the garlic. Peel away some of the papery skins from each head. Lightly ease each head apart, but make sure the cloves remain attached. Sit the heads on a doubled sheet of kitchen foil and bring the foil up to form a parcel. Pour in 45ml | 3 tbsp water and close the parcel. Seal, place in the roasting pan with the chicken, and put the pan in the oven.

3 After 45 minutes, remove the roasting pan from the oven, lift out and open the parcel of garlic and set it on a baking dish. Return the chicken to the oven and cook for another 15 minutes, or until starting to go brown. Test the chicken to see if it is cooked, by inserting a skewer into the thickest part of the thigh. If the juices run clear, it is cooked, but if they are still pink, cook for another 10–15 minutes. Allow the bird to rest in the turned off oven for 15 minutes before carving.

4 Remove the chicken from the oven and pour any juices caught in the cavity into the pan. Serve the chicken with the cooking juices and the roasted garlic.

Pan-fried chicken, served with warm pesto, makes a deliciously quick main course. Serve with pasta or noodles and braised vegetables.

PAN-FRIED CHICKEN with PESTO

INGREDIENTS
serves four

15ml | 1 tbsp olive oil

4 skinless, boneless chicken breast portions

fresh basil leaves, to garnish

braised baby carrots and celery, to serve

for the pesto

90ml | 6 tbsp olive oil

50g | 2oz | 1/2 cup pine nuts

50g | 2oz | 2/3 cup freshly grated Parmesan cheese

50g | 2oz | 1 cup fresh basil leaves

15g | 1/2oz | 1/4 cup fresh parsley

2 garlic cloves, crushed

salt and freshly ground black pepper

1 Heat the oil in a frying pan. Add the chicken breast portions and cook gently for 15–20 minutes, turning several times until they are tender, lightly browned and thoroughly cooked.

2 Meanwhile, make the pesto. Place the olive oil, pine nuts, Parmesan cheese, basil leaves, parsley, garlic and seasoning in a blender or food processor. Process until mixed well together and the required texture is achieved.

3 When cooked, remove the chicken from the pan, cover and keep hot. Reduce the heat slightly, then add the pesto to the pan and cook gently for a few minutes, stirring constantly, until the pesto has warmed through.

4 Pour the warm pesto over the chicken and garnish with basil leaves. Serve with braised baby carrots and celery.

This is a very easy dish to make and looks extremely impressive. It is great for entertaining, as you can get several tenderloins on a barbecue. Serve with a chickpea salad topped with finely chopped onions and parsley, and flavoured with a really mustardy dressing.

BASIL and PECORINO STUFFED PORK

1 Make a 1cm | ½in slit down the length of one of the tenderloins. Continue to slice, cutting along the fold of the meat, until you can open it out flat. Lay between two sheets of baking parchment and pound with a rolling pin to an even thickness of about 1cm | ½in. Lift off the top sheet of parchment and brush the meat with a little oil. Press half the basil leaves on to the surface, then scatter over half the Pecorino cheese and chilli flakes. Add a little pepper.

2 Roll up lengthways to form a sausage and tie with kitchen string (twine). Repeat with the second tenderloin. Put them in a shallow bowl with the remaining oil, cover and put in a cool place until ready to cook.

3 Prepare the barbecue. Twenty minutes before you are ready to cook, season the meat with salt. Wipe any excess oil off the meat. Once the flames have died down, rake the hot coals to one side and insert a drip tray flat beside them so that the cooking temperature can be varied. Position a lightly oiled rack over the coals to heat.

4 When the coals are hot, or covered with a light coating of ash, put the tenderloins on to the heated rack. Cook for 5 minutes over the coals, turning to sear on all sides, then move them over the drip tray and cook for 15 minutes more. Cover with a lid or tented heavy-duty foil, and turn them over from time to time. When done, remove and wrap in foil. Leave to rest for 10 minutes before slicing into rounds and serving.

COOK'S TIP If you don't use a lid and drip tray, move the coals so these are less on one side than the other. Move the pork frequently during cooking to prevent burning.

INGREDIENTS
serves six to eight

2 pork tenderloins, each about 350g | 12oz

45ml | 3 tbsp olive oil

40g | 1½oz | 1½ cups fresh basil leaves, chopped

50g | 2oz Pecorino cheese, grated

2.5ml | ½ tsp chilli flakes

salt and freshly ground black pepper

Known as souvlakia, this used to be street food par excellence in Athens. Lamb makes the best souvlakia but in Greece this has now largely been replaced by pork, which is considerably cheaper. Serve with a large mixed leaf or tomato salad and crusty bread.

SKEWERED LAMB

1 Ask your butcher to trim the meat and cut it into 4cm|1¹/₂in cubes. A little fat is desirable with souvlakia, as it keeps them moist and succulent during cooking. Separate the onion quarters into pieces, each composed of two or three layers, and slice each pepper quarter in half widthways.

2 Put the oil, lemon juice, garlic and herbs in a large bowl. Season with salt and pepper and whisk well to combine. Add the meat cubes, stirring to coat them in the mixture.

3 Cover the bowl tightly and leave to marinate for 4–8 hours in the refrigerator, stirring several times.

4 Lift the meat cubes, reserving the marinade, and thread them on long metal skewers, alternating each piece of meat with a piece of pepper and a piece of onion. Lay them across a grill (broiling) pan or baking tray and brush them with the reserved marinade.

5 Preheat a grill (broiler) until hot or prepare a barbecue. Cook the souvlakia under a medium to high heat or over the hot coals for 10 minutes, until they start to get scorched. If using the grill, do not place them too close to the heat source. Turn the skewers over, brush them again with the marinade (or a little olive oil) and cook them for 10–15 minutes more. Serve immediately, with the salad, chillies and bread.

COOK'S TIP If you are cooking the souvlakia on the barbecue you may need to cook them for slightly longer, depending on the intensity of the heat.

INGREDIENTS
serves four

1 small shoulder of lamb, boned and with most of the fat removed

2–3 onions, preferably red onions, quartered

2 red or green (bell) peppers, quartered and seeded

75ml|5 tbsp extra virgin olive oil

juice of 1 lemon

2 garlic cloves, crushed

5ml|1 tsp dried oregano

2.5ml|¹/₂ tsp dried thyme or some sprigs of fresh thyme, chopped

salt and freshly ground black pepper

mixed leaf or tomato salad, chillies and crusty bread, to serve

This traditional Thai dish – known as yam nua yang – is a great way to liven up a salad. Serve as a light main course on a sultry evening in the garden.

THAI BEEF SALAD

INGREDIENTS
serves four

675g | 1¹/₂lb fillet steak (beef tenderloin) or rump (round) steak

30ml | 2 tbsp olive oil

2 small mild red chillies, seeded and sliced

225g | 8oz | 3¹/₄ cups shiitake mushrooms, sliced

for the dressing

3 spring onions (scallions), finely chopped

2 garlic cloves, finely chopped

juice of 1 lime

15–30ml | 1–2 tbsp fish or oyster sauce

5ml | 1 tsp soft light brown sugar

30ml | 2 tbsp chopped fresh coriander (cilantro)

to serve

1 cos or romaine lettuce, torn into strips

175g | 6oz cherry tomatoes, halved

5cm | 2in piece cucumber, peeled, halved and thinly sliced

45ml | 3 tbsp toasted sesame seeds

1 Preheat the grill (broiler) until hot, then cook the steak for 2–4 minutes on each side, depending on how well done you like it. (In Thailand, the beef is traditionally served quite rare.) Leave to cool for at least 15 minutes.

2 Use a very sharp knife to slice the meat as thinly as possible and place the slices in a bowl.

3 Heat the olive oil in a small frying pan. Add the red chillies and the sliced mushrooms and cook for 5 minutes, stirring occasionally. Turn off the heat and add the steak slices to the pan, then stir well to coat the slices in the chilli and mushroom mixture.

4 Mix all the ingredients for the dressing together in a bowl, then pour over the meat mixture and toss gently.

5 Arrange the salad ingredients on a serving plate. Spoon the warm steak mixture in the centre and sprinkle the sesame seeds over. Serve immediately.

VARIATION If you can find them, yellow chillies make a colourful addition to this dish. Substitute one for one of the red chillies. This warm salad method works well whatever the green leaves you have to hand.

Sweet and Sensuous

There are so many flowers and herbs to scent
and flavour food at this verdant time of year.
Try the heady taste of lavender, flavour with
elderflowers or decorate with rose petals.
There is something very satisfying in using
produce from your own, or someone else's, garden.

Rosewater-scented cream and fresh raspberries form the filling for this delectable dessert. Though they look impressive, these shortcakes are easy to make.

RASPBERRY and ROSE PETAL SHORTCAKES

INGREDIENTS
serves six

115g | 4oz | 1/2 cup unsalted (sweet) butter, softened

50g | 2oz | 1/4 cup caster (superfine) sugar

1/2 vanilla pod, split, seeds reserved

115g | 4oz | 1 cup plain (all-purpose) flour, plus extra for dusting

50g | 2oz | 1/3 cup semolina

icing (confectioners') sugar, for dusting

for the filling

300ml | 1/2 pint | 1 1/4 cups double (heavy) cream

15ml | 1 tbsp icing (confectioners') sugar

2.5ml | 1/2 tsp rosewater

450g | 1lb | 4 cups raspberries

for the decoration

12 miniature roses, unsprayed

6 mint sprigs

1 egg white, beaten

caster (superfine) sugar, for dusting

1 Cream the butter, caster sugar and vanilla seeds in a bowl until pale and fluffy. Sift the flour and semolina together, then gradually work the dry ingredients into the creamed mixture to make a biscuit dough. Gently knead the dough on a lightly floured surface until smooth. Roll out quite thinly and prick all over with a fork. Using a 7.5cm | 3in fluted cutter, cut out 12 rounds. Place these on a baking sheet and chill for 30 minutes.

2 Meanwhile, make the filling. Whisk the cream with the icing sugar until soft peaks form. Fold in the rosewater and chill until required.

3 Preheat the oven to 180°C | 350°F | Gas 4. To make the decoration, paint the roses and mint leaves with the egg white. Dust with sugar and dry on a wire rack.

4 Bake the shortcakes for 15 minutes or until lightly golden. Lift them off the baking sheet with a metal spatula and cool on a wire rack.

5 To assemble the shortcakes, spoon the rosewater cream on to half the biscuits. Add a layer of raspberries, then top with a second shortcake. Dust with icing sugar. Decorate with the frosted roses and mint sprigs.

COOK'S TIP For best results, serve the shortcakes as soon as possible after assembling them, otherwise they are likely to turn soggy from the berries' liquid.

VARIATIONS Other soft red summer berries, such as mulberries, loganberries and tayberries, would be equally good in this dessert.

Desserts don't come much easier than this – fresh figs in crisp filo pastry, with a creamy almond batter. The tart tastes wonderful served with cream or yogurt.

FRESH FIG FILO TART

1 Preheat the oven to 190°C|375°F|Gas 5. Grease a 25 x 16cm|10 x 6¼in baking tin (pan) with butter. Brush each filo sheet in turn with melted butter and use to line the tin.

2 Trim the excess pastry, leaving a little overhanging the edge. Arrange the figs over the base of the tart.

3 Sift the flour into a bowl and stir in the caster sugar. Add the eggs and a little of the milk and whisk until smooth. Gradually whisk in the remaining milk and the almond essence. Pour the batter over the figs.

4 Bake for 1 hour or until the batter has set and is golden. Remove the tart from the oven and allow it to cool in the tin on a wire rack for 10 minutes. Dust with the icing sugar and serve with cream, yogurt or large scoops of fresh vanilla flavoured ice cream.

INGREDIENTS
serves six to eight

5 sheets of filo pastry, each measuring 35 x 25cm|14 x 10in, thawed if frozen

25g|1oz|2 tbsp butter, melted

6 fresh figs, cut into wedges

75g|3oz|¾ cup plain (all-purpose) flour

75g|3oz|6 tbsp caster (superfine) sugar

4 eggs

450ml|¾ pint|scant 2 cups creamy milk

2.5ml|½ tsp almond essence (extract)

15ml|1 tbsp icing (confectioners') sugar, for dusting

whipped cream, Greek (US strained plain) yogurt or vanilla ice cream, to serve.

This fresh fruit salad, with its special colour and exotic flavour, is a refreshing way to end a meal. It is a great dish to serve on a day when it is too hot to cook.

SCENTED RED and ORANGE FRUIT SALAD

INGREDIENTS
serves four to six

350–400g | 12–14oz | 3–3¹/₂ cups strawberries, hulled and halved

3 oranges, peeled and segmented

3 small blood oranges, peeled and segmented

1–2 passion fruit

120ml | 4fl oz | ¹/₂ cup dry white wine

sugar, to taste

1 Put the strawberries and oranges into a serving bowl. Halve the passion fruit and spoon the flesh into the bowl.

2 Pour the wine over the fruit and add sugar to taste. Toss gently and then chill until ready to serve.

VARIATIONS: Other fruits that can be added include pear, kiwi fruit and banana. Tropical fruits like pomegranate or slices of starfruit add a decorative touch.

Take advantage of the short apricot season by making this charming apricot and almond dessert, delicately scented with lemon juice and orange flower water.

APRICOTS with ALMOND PASTE

1 Preheat the oven to 180°C | 350°F | Gas 4. Place the sugar, lemon juice and water in a small pan and heat gently, stirring constantly, until the sugar has all dissolved. Bring to the boil and simmer gently for 5–10 minutes to make a thin syrup.

2 Place the ground almonds, icing sugar, orange flower water, butter and almond essence in a bowl and blend together to make a smooth paste.

3 Wash the apricots and then make a slit in the flesh and ease out the stone (pit). Take small pieces of the almond paste, roll into balls and press one into each of the apricots.

4 Arrange the stuffed apricots in a shallow ovenproof dish and carefully pour the sugar syrup around them. Cover with foil and bake in the oven for 25–30 minutes.

5 Serve the apricots with a little of the syrup and decorated with sprigs of fresh mint.

COOK'S TIP Always use a heavy pan when making syrup and stir constantly with a wooden spoon until the sugar has completely dissolved. Do not let the liquid come to the boil before it has dissolved, or the result will be grainy.

INGREDIENTS
serves six

75g | 3oz | 6 tbsp caster (superfine) sugar

30ml | 2 tbsp lemon juice

300ml | 1/2 pint | 1 1/4 cups water

115g | 4oz | 1 cup ground almonds

50g | 2oz | 1/2 cup icing (confectioners') sugar

a little orange flower water

25g | 1oz | 2 tbsp unsalted (sweet) butter, melted

2.5ml | 1/2 tsp almond essence (extract)

900g | 2lb fresh apricots

fresh mint sprigs, to decorate

No book of seasonal cooking would be complete without this well-loved, classic recipe. Although easy to make it is always an impressive centrepiece.

SUMMER PUDDING

INGREDIENTS
serves four to six

8 x 1cm | 1/2in thick slices of day-old white bread, crusts removed

800g | 1³/₄lb | 6–7 cups mixed berry fruit, such as strawberries, raspberries, blackcurrants, redcurrants and blueberries

50g | 2oz | 1/4 cup golden caster (superfine) sugar

lightly whipped double (heavy) cream or crème fraîche, to serve

1 Trim a slice of bread to fit in the base of a 1.2 litre | 2 pint | 5 cup bowl, then trim another 5–6 slices to line the sides of the bowl.

2 Place all the fruit in a pan with the sugar. Cook gently for 4–5 minutes until the juices begin to run – it will not be necessary to add any water. Allow the mixture to cool slightly, then spoon the berries and enough of their juices to moisten into the bread-lined bowl. Save any leftover juice to serve with the dessert.

3 Fold over the excess bread, then cover the fruit with the remaining bread slices, trimming them to fit. Place a small plate or saucer directly on top, fitting it inside the bowl. Weight it with a 900g | 2lb weight if you have one, or use a couple of full cans.

4 Leave the bowl in the refrigerator for at least 8 hours or overnight. To serve, run a knife between the dessert and the bowl and turn it out on to a plate. Spoon any reserved juices over the top and serve with whipped cream or crème fraîche.

Delicately perfumed with just a hint of lavender, this delightful, pastel pink sorbet is perfect for a special occasion dinner.

STRAWBERRY and LAVENDER SORBET

INGREDIENTS
serves six

150g | 5oz | 3/4 cup caster (superfine) sugar

300ml | 1/2 pint | 1 1/4 cups water

6 fresh lavender flowers

500g | 1 1/4lb | 5 cups strawberries, hulled

1 egg white

lavender flowers, to decorate

1 Put the sugar and water into a pan and heat gently, stirring constantly, until the sugar has completely dissolved. Bring to the boil, remove from the heat, add the lavender flowers and leave to steep for 1 hour. Strain and, if time, chill the syrup before using.

2 Purée the strawberries in a food processor or in batches in a blender, then press the purée through a large sieve into a bowl.

3 BY HAND: Spoon the purée into a plastic tub or similar freezerproof container, mix in the lavender syrup and freeze for 4 hours, or until the mixture is mushy.
USING AN ICE CREAM MAKER: Pour the strawberry purée into the bowl of an ice cream maker and mix in the lavender syrup. Churn for 20 minutes, or until the mixture is thick.

4 Whisk the egg white until it just turns frothy.
BY HAND: Scoop the sorbet (sherbet) from the tub into a food processor, process it until smooth, then add the egg white. Spoon the sorbet back into the tub and freeze for 4 hours, or until firm.
USING AN ICE CREAM MAKER: Add the egg white to the ice cream maker and continue to churn until the sorbet (sherbet) is firm enough to scoop.

5 Serve the sorbet in scoops, decorated with lavender flowers.

COOK'S TIP The size of lavender flowers varies. If they are very small, you may need to use eight instead of six. To double check, taste a little of the cooled lavender syrup. If you think the flavour is a little mild, add 2–3 more flowers, reheat and cool again before using.

A classic combination that makes a really refreshing sorbet. Make it in summer as a stunning finale to an *al fresco* meal.

GOOSEBERRY and ELDERFLOWER SORBET

1 Put 30ml | 2 tbsp of the sugar in a large pan with 30ml | 2 tbsp of the water. Set aside. Mix the remaining sugar and water in a separate heavy pan. Heat gently, stirring constantly, until the sugar has dissolved. Bring to the boil and boil for 1 minute, without stirring, to make a syrup.

2 Remove from the heat and add the elderflower heads, pressing them into the syrup with a wooden spoon. Leave to steep for about 1 hour.

3 Strain the elderflower syrup through a sieve placed over a bowl. Set the syrup aside. Add the gooseberries to the pan containing the reserved sugar and water. Cover and cook very gently for about 5 minutes, until the gooseberries have softened.

4 Transfer to a food processor or blender and add the apple juice. Process until smooth, then press through a sieve into a bowl. Leave to cool. Stir in the elderflower syrup and green food colouring, if using. Chill until very cold.

5 BY HAND: Pour the mixture into a shallow container and freeze until thick, preferably overnight.
USING AN ICE CREAM MAKER: Churn the mixture until it holds its shape. Transfer to a freezerproof container and freeze for several hours or overnight.

6 To decorate the serving glasses, put a little egg white in a shallow bowl and a thin layer of caster sugar on a flat plate. Dip the rim of each glass in the egg white, then the sugar, to coat evenly. Leave to dry. Scoop the sorbet (sherbet) carefully into the glasses, decorate with elderflowers and serve.

INGREDIENTS
serves six

150g | 5oz | ⅔ cup caster (superfine) sugar

175ml | 6fl oz | ¼ cup water

10 elderflower heads, plus a few extra, to decorate

500g | 1¼lb | 4 cups gooseberries

200ml | 7fl oz | scant 1 cup apple juice

dash of green food colouring (optional)

a little beaten egg white and caster sugar, to decorate

Autumn Cooking

INTRODUCTION

As bright summer hues mellow to a glow, the flavours and aromas of produce seem to mature to a rounded richness. Sedate autumn provides a harvest of fruit, vegetables and leaves that is less demanding than the fast-growing summer glut. There are plump, crisp cabbages; firm roots and tubers; crunchy apples and juicy pears. In many rural areas astounding pyramids of golden pumpkins take on sculptural forms at farm gates and in farmers' markets. Slightly smaller pumpkins and squashes make a correspondingly dramatic impact on supermarket displays.

Against a backcloth of smoke from gently smouldering leaves, gardeners unearth substantial root vegetables. The weather is perfect for pottering in the kitchen garden – neither hot enough to laze, nor cold enough for hand-clapping and foot-stamping. The tangled remnants of summer growth are cleared to reveal big vegetables and firm fruit with well-defined flavours – perfect for complementing the season's meats.

For food shopping, the change from summer to autumn is a metamorphosis rather than a sudden switch. Chunky root vegetables become cheaper, and there is a good choice of apples and pears from local orchards. Supermarket meat displays offer braising and stewing cuts, while butchers dealing in game display the new season's birds to good effect in their windows.

Warming dishes

One of the pleasures of autumn cooking is its relaxed pace, when evenings at home begin to seem like a good idea. Warmer foods become appealing – mellow casseroles, creamy mash, moist risottos, baked soufflés and soothing soups. It may not yet be cool enough for steaming porridge, but warm buns and breads are welcome alternatives or additions to breakfast fruit salads and yogurts. Country walks provide opportunities for

rummaging among the brambles for juicy fruit, gathering nuts and picking mushrooms. Traditionally, going home for tea meant that there was probably teabread or fruit loaf to sample, because autumn is the time of year when there is renewed enthusiasm for baking, keeping the house warm with a constant supply of heat and delicious aromas.

Seasonal celebrations

A good harvest is usually celebrated by sharing meals and distributing produce to the community. Festivities take over on Halloween, bonfire night and Thanksgiving, providing opportunities for fun parties. Fancy dress or cool-weather barbecues are informal, with sizzling-hot sausages and chargrilled baked potatoes accompanied by steaming mugs of golden pumpkin soup. Toffee apples, gooey apple cakes and oaty flapjacks are sweet treats.

Storing for winter

Autumn is the time for squirrelling away winter stores. Pickles and chutneys are just right for using apples, pears, crisp red cabbage and those leftover tomatoes that will not ripen on the windowsill. Chutneys, pickles and clear jellies, made from quinces or crab apples, for instance, are the perfect complement to cold meat cuts and cheeses.

A glut of apples or pears can be preserved by wrapping each fruit in paper and storing in a cool and dark place. Root vegetables can be saved in sand or sawdust. Onions and garlic bulbs can be strung up and hung for use even later in the year. Stringing is an excellent way to ensure that alliums stay dry and well ventilated, and they will still be good the following spring if kept in a frost-free place.

Hedgerow pickings

One of the traditional pleasures of autumn is the gathering of nature's free harvest. Country dwellers have long benefited from fruit from the hedgerows and fungi from the ground. Domestic traditions for when and how to pick are passed down through generations and matched by recipes for jams and pickles.

FINE FRUIT

Prize pickings are found high on the hedges and branches exposed to the sun. The right rainfall produces plump fruit – succulent blackberries on tangled brambles; bright clusters of rowan berries high in mountain ash trees; glowing rose hips on thorny climbers; and astringent little wild crab apples. The best and sweetest blackberries are big and tender, and they taste wonderful freshly picked, with sugar and cream. They can also be poached, used in baked desserts or made into jams and jellies.

Rowan berries, rose hips and crab apples throw off their bitter guise and burst into flavour when cooked or crushed. Straining and sweetening releases and enhances the fruity essence, which is superb in syrups and preserves. Sour sloes and tart damsons also taste fabulous in all sorts of cooked dishes. Sloe gin is especially good: each fruit has to be well pricked (traditionally, with a silver needle) before being macerated in spirit.

NICE NUTS

Trees laden with hazelnuts are irresistible to wildlife and human gatherers alike. Those who are accustomed to spotting the little clusters of brown shells hidden between speckled leaves usually enjoy them young, crisp and moist, while they are still slightly under-ripe. Any nuts that survive undiscovered on the branches to mature are fuller in flavour. They can be stored in cool, dry conditions for later in the year.

MARVELLOUS MUSHROOMS

Wild mushrooms seem to make a miraculous appearance in autumn. When the weather is just right – neither too wet, nor too dry – weird and wonderful fungi seem to grow almost overnight, ready to be plucked with care from open fields or from beneath the ground cover of autumn leaves.

Experienced fungi foragers exercise knowledge and respect, understanding that many edible fungi are partnered by poisonous look-alikes. They treat each species with care, selecting only the examples they know to be safe. And the crop is always respected, never ravaged, for rough lifting and overpicking destroy the fragile equilibrium of renewal. Please consult an authoritative guide before eating any fungi.

Preparing wild mushrooms requires a little patience to remove dirt. This involves gently wiping, cleaning with a soft brush, or swirling in water, but never soaking. A network of tiny holes is the tell-tale sign that bugs may be present; trimming off small areas usually disposes of unwanted pests. Fungi that are riddled with holes must be discarded, so the trick is to spot bad attacks while picking and leave the fungi in the wild to grow and reproduce.

Drying is one method of preserving wild mushrooms. The traditional method is to thread the mushrooms on string and hang them in a dry, warm and airy place to dry slowly. They can also be dried in electric fan-assisted dryers or on racks in a very cool oven. To store the fungi in a container (rather than strung up in a suitable area), they must be thoroughly dried or they will go mouldy. When completely dry, they can be stored in airtight containers in a cool, dark cupboard indefinitely.

Drying changes the character of wild fungi ingredients, transforming them from lightly flavoured foods requiring minimal cooking, to concentrated ingredients with condiment-like qualities. Dried mushrooms can bring an intense richness to sauces, casseroles and risottos.

Harvest highlights

Orchard fruit, squashes and grains are good at this time of year and pumpkins are an essential feature. Large main crop potatoes have thick skins that become deliciously crisp when baked; with buttery, fluffy centres, they are a firm favourite.

TERRIFIC ROOTS AND STEMS

Main-crop carrots, swedes (rutabagas) and the first of the parsnips are piled on vegetable stalls and in supermarkets. However, traditionally parsnips are not considered to be at their best until they have had a dose of frost in the ground. Celeriac and Jerusalem artichokes are two delicately flavoured ground vegetables to seek out.

Celeriac is not strictly a root but the swollen stem base (or corm) of the plant. It has a mild celery flavour and a slightly crunchy texture. The large, unevenly surfaced bulb should be peeled and then sliced or diced for cooking. It is good raw or cooked, especially in soup, puréed or poached in a little white wine and stock. Boil and mash celeriac with potatoes to make a creamy accompaniment for grilled fish.

Jerusalem artichokes are also delicate, but with a nutty flavour. They are incredibly easy to grow and provide a generous crop. Modern cultivars are not as rugged and knobbly as the older ones, so they are easier to scrub. The flesh is crisp and rather thin in texture, becoming watery if overcooked. Jerusalem artichokes have a reputation for causing flatulence, especially when made into soup. This is because they contain inulin, a type of fructose that is indigestible. Inulin is soluble, so some is lost in discarded cooking water but, of course, not when both vegetables and cooking liquid make soup. The flavour may be splendid, but to those who find artichokes a problem, the side effects are unpleasant. Par-boiling in their skins, then tossing with a little oil and roasting works well. Peeling and simmering for five minutes before slicing is another good starting point. The slices are delicious sautéed or drizzled with a little cream, sprinkled lightly with breadcrumbs and baked until golden.

IMPRESSIVE PUMPKINS

Many people are intimidated by the sheer size of pumpkins and afraid they may run short of ideas or tire of pumpkin pie or soup. There is no need to worry though, as the pumpkin is such a versatile vegetable. There will always be extra to cook with after the traditional lanterns have been carved.

- Slice the top off a small pumpkin and scoop out the seeds. Replace the top and bake, wrapped in foil. Scoop out and purée the tender flesh with good stock and cream to make a silky soup. Reheat without boiling, then season with chopped chives and nutmeg.

- Steam or boil wedges or cubes of pumpkin until just tender for gratins and pies. Cook until soft for purée. Add to vegetable stews and serve with couscous.

- Diced pumpkin makes excellent chutney or pickle.

GOOD SEEDS AND GRAINS

There are lots of delicious ways to use oats, barley, wheat and rye flakes, not just in baking breads and cakes. Containing the vitamins and minerals found in most seeds, they provide a healthy addition to any diet.

- Dry-roast flaked grains in a heavy pan over a low heat, stirring until lightly browned. Cook each type separately, then mix together. Roast sesame, sunflower and pumpkin seeds in separate batches and add to the grains. Use in muesli (granola), bread doughs, as a gratin topping, in salads or sprinkled over soup.

- Add oat flakes to crumble mix for topping apples or other fruit.

- Rolled or flaked oats are convenient and easy for thickening soup. Stir them into the soup while bringing to the boil. Simmer for a few minutes, until thick.

APPLES AND PEARS

Cooking apples become soft and pulpy during cooking. They are good for apple sauce, purée and chutney. Eating apples become tender but stay whole when cooked. They are good poached, baked or used in tarte tatin. Apples and pears discolour quickly when cut and peeled. To prevent this, place the fruit in a bowl of water with a good squeeze of lemon juice.

- Poach halved, peeled and cored eating apples in cider syrup with 3–4 green cardamom pods until tender. Reduce the syrup to a small amount of golden glaze to coat the apples before serving warm.

- Poach whole, peeled eating apples or pears until tender. Cool, then drain, and remove their cores. Fill the cavity with marzipan, wrap in filo pastry and bake until crisp and golden.

Seasonal baking

Hearty breads and flavour-packed preserves are signature dishes of the season. Together they complement hard or soft cheese, baked ham and cured meats. Sweet-sour pickles and crusty bread also go very well with thick seasonal soups.

RAISING BREAD

The aroma of freshly baked bread, raised with yeast, is unbeatable. There are several types of yeast. Fresh yeast is beige and moist but firm, with a crumbly "squeaky" texture – it is mixed with a little warm liquid and allowed to become frothy before it is added to the dough. The dough must rise twice. Ordinary dried yeast is sprinkled over warm liquid and allowed to rehydrate and become frothy. Fast-action dried yeast is added to dry ingredients. Instead of the traditional double rising, the dough is shaped and allowed to prove or rise once only.

- Use milk instead of water to make a slightly richer bread with a deep golden crust.

- Soda bread is quick and easy. Bicarbonate of soda (baking soda) is used as the raising agent, with buttermilk to mix or lemon juice added to the dough.

- Savoury scone (biscuit) dough uses baking powder or a mixture of bicarbonate of soda and cream of tartar as a raising agent. Mixed dried herbs or oregano and finely chopped sundried tomatoes taste good in scones, especially with a little freshly grated Parmesan.

- Packet dough mix is a good base for flavoured bread. Add roasted fennel or caraway seeds to white bread mix or chopped walnuts to wholemeal (whole-wheat) mix.

- Add mixed dried fruit to dough to transform plain bread into a fruit loaf.

Preserving

Chutneys and pickles are hassle-free preserves – easy to make, safe to store and versatile in use. They are convenient store-cupboard (pantry) condiments and well suited to contemporary cooking and eating.

Vinegar and sugar are the preserving agents. Classic chutneys are simmered gently for hours until thick and pulpy. Pickles are cooked for a shorter period, until tender but still chunky. Some pickles are simply raw or poached fruit or vegetables immersed in vinegar or vinegar syrup; the pickling liquor is not consumed.

Whole or ground spices are typical flavouring ingredients – coriander, cloves, allspice, fennel seeds, chillies and/or ground ginger. Onions are essential, garlic is widely used, and fresh root ginger occasionally contributes its inimitable zest.

- Whole spices contribute a cleaner flavour than their ground counterparts. Tie them in a piece of muslin (cheesecloth) to remove them easily from a pickle or chutney after cooking. Crushed spices and small whole seeds contribute texture to pickles.

- For smooth, mellow chutneys, simmer the mixture gently until soft before adding the sugar, then continue cooking very slowly until rich and thick.

- The longer the preserve is cooked once the sugar is added, the richer, darker and more caramelized it becomes.

- Dried fruits, such as dates, raisins and apricots, are used whole, chunky or chopped for their flavour and sweetness.

STORING, MATURING AND USING

Pots with vinegar-proof lids are essential, otherwise the vinegar attacks and breaks down exposed metal, spoiling the preserve. Jars should be thoroughly washed in sterilizing solution and warmed. Pot cooked preserves immediately, covering them while they are hot for a good, clean seal.

All chutneys and pickles should be matured for at least a couple of weeks before eating, preferably for one month. As the vinegar and spices mellow, the preserve becomes less harsh and more intriguing in flavour. Stored in a cool, dark and dry place, they keep for 6–12 months.

- Serve preserves with cheese and cooked meats. Spread them in sandwiches – sweet-sour pickle goes especially well with smooth peanut butter.

- Offer chunky pumpkin pickle with rich pâtés or terrines.

- Ginger-seasoned pickles are good with roasted carrots or swirled into smooth, rich carrot or parsnip soup.

- Light pickles, with the sugar added fairly late in the cooking process, are delicious in salad dressings for chunks of cooked chicken or ham.

Warm and Comforting

As autumn arrives and the days get shorter and cooler, relaxing meals at home become appealing. The season has come for curling up with comforting food after a country walk or afternoons spent in the garden tending a bonfire. Enjoy hearty soups, savoury pastries and pâtés, warm salads and hot seafood as appetizers or as satisfying side dishes.

Lentils are an autumn staple. As they do not need soaking, they make an easy option for a quick meal. The secret of good lentil soup is to be generous with the olive oil.

LENTIL and TOMATO SOUP

INGREDIENTS
serves four

275g | 10oz | 1¼ cups brown-green lentils, preferably the small variety

150ml | ¼ pint | ⅔ cup extra virgin olive oil

1 onion, thinly sliced

2 garlic cloves, sliced into thin batons

1 carrot, sliced into thin discs

400g | 14oz can chopped tomatoes

15ml | 1 tbsp tomato purée (paste)

2.5ml | ½ tsp dried oregano

1 litre | 1¾ pints | 4 cups hot water

salt and ground black pepper

30ml | 2 tbsp roughly chopped fresh herb leaves, to garnish

1 Rinse the lentils, drain them and put them in a large pan with cold water to cover. Bring to the boil and boil for 3–4 minutes. Strain, discarding the liquid, and set the lentils aside.

2 Wipe the pan clean, heat the olive oil in it, then add the onion and sauté until translucent. Stir in the garlic and, as soon as it becomes aromatic, return the lentils to the pan. Add the carrot, tomatoes, tomato purée and oregano. Stir in the hot water and a little pepper to taste.

3 Bring to the boil, then lower the heat, cover the pan and cook gently for 20–30 minutes until the lentils feel soft but have not begun to disintegrate. Add salt and the chopped herbs just before serving.

COOK'S TIP This recipe uses staples from the pantry. Serve with fresh warm bread and cheese to complement the flavours and to make a filling and hearty meal. If you still have a few remaining herbs in the kitchen garden, such as sage or rosemary, these can be used to replace the dried oregano.

This silky, smooth and nutty soup with hints of smoky bacon is so easy to make. Enjoy it with a bowl of warmed tortilla chips, spiced-up with extra paprika and cumin.

BACON and CHICKPEA SOUP

1 Drain the chickpeas, put them in a large pan and cover with plenty of cold water. Bring to the boil and simmer for about 20 minutes. Strain and set aside.

2 Melt the butter in a large pan and add the pancetta or streaky bacon. Fry over a medium heat until just beginning to turn golden. Add the chopped vegetables and cook for 5–10 minutes until soft.

3 Add the chickpeas to the pan, with the chopped rosemary, bay leaves, halved garlic cloves and enough water to cover completely. Bring to the boil, half cover, turn down the heat and simmer for 45–60 minutes, stirring occasionally. (The chickpeas should start to disintegrate and will thicken the soup.)

4 Allow the soup to cool slightly, then pour it into a blender or food processor and process until smooth. Return the soup to the rinsed-out pan, taste and season with salt and plenty of black pepper. Reheat gently.

5 To make the tortilla chips, preheat the oven to 180°C | 350°F | Gas 4. Melt the butter with the paprika and cumin in a pan, then lightly brush the mixture over the tortilla chips. Reserve any left over spiced butter. Spread the chips out on a baking sheet and warm through in the oven for 5 minutes.

6 Ladle the soup into bowls, pour some reserved spiced butter over each serving and sprinkle with a little paprika. Serve with the warm tortilla chips.

INGREDIENTS
serves four to six

400g | 14oz | 2 cups dried chickpeas, soaked overnight in cold water

115g | 4oz | 1/2 cup butter

150g | 5oz pancetta or streaky (fatty) bacon, roughly chopped

2 onions, finely chopped

1 carrot, chopped

1 celery stick, chopped

15ml | 1 tbsp chopped fresh rosemary

2 fresh bay leaves

2 garlic cloves, halved

salt and ground black pepper

for the tortilla chips

75g | 3oz | 6 tbsp butter

2.5ml | 1/2 tsp sweet paprika

1.5ml | 1/4 tsp ground cumin

175g | 6oz plain tortilla chips

Pine nuts are the seeds that come from the cones of the *Pinus pinea* tree. Their delicate nutty taste is a marvellous foil to the feta cheese in these parcels. Offer round with drinks or present as part of a large meal or buffet table.

HALF-MOON CHEESE PIES with PINE NUTS

INGREDIENTS
makes twelve to fourteen

1 large (US extra large) egg, plus 1 egg yolk for glazing

150g | 5oz feta cheese

30ml | 2 tbsp milk

30ml | 2 tbsp chopped fresh mint leaves

15ml | 1 tbsp raisins

15 ml | 1 tbsp pine nuts, lightly toasted

a little vegetable oil, for greasing

for the pastry

225g | 8oz | 2 cups self-raising (self-rising) flour

45ml | 3 tbsp extra virgin olive oil

15g | 1/2oz | 1 tbsp butter, melted

90g | 31/2oz Greek (US strained plain) yogurt

1 To make the pastry, put the flour in a bowl and mix in the oil, butter and yogurt by hand. Cover and rest in the refrigerator for 15 minutes.

2 Meanwhile, make the filling. Beat the egg lightly in a bowl. Crumble in the cheese, then mix in the milk, mint, raisins and pine nuts.

3 Preheat the oven to 190°C | 375°F | Gas 5. Cover half of the pastry, thinly roll out the remainder and cut out 7.5cm | 3in rounds.

4 Place a heaped teaspoon of filling on each round and fold the pastry over to make a half-moon shape. Press the edges to seal, then place the pies on a greased baking sheet. Repeat with the remaining pastry. Brush the pies with egg yolk and bake for 20 minutes, or until golden.

This pâté is particularly good made with the new season's walnuts, sometimes known as "wet" walnuts, which are available in the early autumn.

ROAST GARLIC with GOAT'S CHEESE PÂTÉ

1 Preheat the oven to 180°C|350°F|Gas 4. Strip the papery skin from the garlic bulbs. Place them in an ovenproof dish large enough to hold them snugly. Tuck in the fresh rosemary sprigs and fresh thyme sprigs, drizzle the olive oil over and season with a little sea salt and plenty of ground black pepper.

2 Cover the garlic tightly with foil and bake in the oven for 50–60 minutes, opening the parcel and basting once halfway through the cooking time. Set aside and leave to cool.

3 Preheat the grill (broiler). To make the pâté, cream the cheese with the thyme, parsley and chopped walnuts. Beat in 15ml|1 tbsp of the cooking oil from the garlic and season to taste with plenty of ground black pepper. Transfer the pâté to a serving bowl and chill until ready to serve.

4 Brush the sourdough bread slices on one side with the remaining cooking oil from the garlic bulbs, then grill (broil) until lightly toasted.

5 Divide the pâté among four individual plates. Drizzle the walnut oil, if using, over the goat's cheese pâté and grind some black pepper over it. Place some garlic on each plate and serve with the pâté and some toasted bread. Garnish the pâté with a little fresh thyme and serve a few freshly shelled walnuts with each portion.

INGREDIENTS
serves four

4 large garlic bulbs

4 fresh rosemary sprigs

8 fresh thyme sprigs

60ml|4 tbsp olive oil

sea salt and ground black pepper

thyme sprigs, to garnish

4–8 slices sourdough bread and walnuts, to serve

for the pâté

200g|7oz|scant 1 cup soft goat's cheese

5ml|1 tsp finely chopped fresh thyme

15ml|1 tbsp chopped fresh parsley

50g|2oz|1/3 cup chopped walnuts

15ml|1 tbsp walnut oil (optional)

fresh thyme, to garnish

Shallot and chives in a creamy dressing add bite to this warm salad of potato and sweet mussels. Serve with flavoursome watercress or mixed-leaf salad, and plenty of freshly baked bread for perfect autumn fare.

POTATO and MUSSEL SALAD

INGREDIENTS
serves four

675g | 1¹/₂lb salad potatoes

1kg | 2¹/₄lb mussels, scrubbed and beards removed

200ml | 7fl oz | scant 1 cup dry white wine

15g | ¹/₂oz flat leaf parsley, chopped

salt and ground black pepper

chopped fresh chives or chive flowers, to garnish

for the dressing

105ml | 7 tbsp mild olive oil

15–30ml | 1–2 tbsp white wine vinegar

5ml | 1 tsp Dijon mustard

1 large shallot, very finely chopped

15ml | 1 tbsp chopped fresh chives

45ml | 3 tbsp double (heavy) cream

pinch of sugar (optional)

1 Cook the potatoes whole in boiling, salted water for 15–20 minutes or until tender. Drain, cool, then peel. Slice the potatoes into a bowl and toss with 30ml | 2 tbsp of the oil for the dressing.

2 Discard any open mussels that do not close when sharply tapped. Bring the white wine to the boil in a large, heavy pan. Add the mussels, cover and boil vigorously for 3–4 minutes, shaking the pan occasionally, until the mussels have opened. Discard any mussels that have not opened after 5 minutes' cooking. Drain and shell the mussels, reserving the cooking liquid.

3 Boil the reserved cooking liquid until reduced to about 45ml | 3 tbsp. Strain this through a fine sieve over the potatoes and toss to mix.

4 For the dressing, whisk together the remaining oil, 15ml | 1tbsp of vinegar, the mustard, shallot and chives.

5 Add the cream and whisk again to form a thick dressing. Adjust the seasoning, adding more vinegar and/or a pinch of sugar to taste.

6 Toss the mussels with the potatoes, then mix in the dressing and chopped parsley. Serve sprinkled with extra chopped chives or chive flowers separated into florets.

COOK'S TIP Potato salads such as this one should not be chilled, as the cold alters the texture of the potatoes and of the creamy dressing. For the best flavour and texture, serve this salad at room temperature.

This is the perfect autumn oyster dish, served bubbling and golden brown. Those who are not "as rich as Rockefeller" can give mussels or clams the same treatment.

OYSTERS ROCKEFELLER

1 Preheat the oven to 220°C | 425°F | Gas 7. Make a bed of coarse salt on two large baking sheets. Set the oysters in the half-shell in the bed of salt to keep them steady. Set aside.

2 Melt the butter in a frying pan. Add the finely chopped shallots and cook them over a low heat for 2–3 minutes until they are softened. Stir in the spinach and let it wilt.

3 Add the parsley, celery leaves and breadcrumbs to the pan and fry gently for 5 minutes. Season with salt, pepper and Tabasco or cayenne.

4 Divide the stuffing among the oysters. Drizzle a few drops of Pernod or Ricard over each oyster, then bake for about 5 minutes, until bubbling and golden brown. Serve on a heated platter on a shallow salt bed with lemon wedges.

COOK'S TIP If you prefer a smoother stuffing, whizz it to a paste in a food processor or blender.

INGREDIENTS
serves six

450g | 1lb | 3 cups coarse salt, plus extra to serve

24 oysters, opened

115g | 4oz | 1/2 cup butter

2 shallots, finely chopped

500g | 1 1/4 lb spinach leaves, finely chopped

60ml | 4 tbsp chopped fresh parsley

60ml | 4 tbsp chopped celery leaves

90ml | 6 tbsp fresh white breadcrumbs

Tabasco sauce or cayenne pepper

10–20ml | 2–4 tsp Pernod or Ricard

salt and ground black pepper

lemon wedges, to serve

Earthy and Delicious

Rich autumnal colours are captured in the ripe pumpkins and squashes which appear in gardens, markets and local shops. Wild mushrooms offer their intense flavour to soufflés and pasta dishes. Chunky root vegetables are abundant too, and they combine brilliantly with the nuttiness of beans, lentils, grains and slowly cooked and caramelized onions or shallots to provide delicious vegetarian options.

The rosemary gives this rich and creamy risotto a sweet pungency, while garlic and chilli add bite.

PUMPKIN, ROSEMARY and CHILLI RISOTTO

INGREDIENTS
serves four

115g | 4oz | 1/2 cup butter

1 small onion, finely chopped

2 large garlic cloves, crushed

1 fresh red chilli, seeded and finely chopped

250g | 9oz fresh pumpkin or butternut squash, peeled and roughly chopped

30ml | 2 tbsp chopped fresh rosemary

250g | 9oz | 1 1/2 cups risotto rice, preferably arborio or Vialone Nano

about 750ml | 1 1/4 pints | 3 cups hot chicken stock, preferably fresh

50g | 2oz | 2/3 cup freshly grated Parmesan cheese, plus extra to serve

salt and ground black pepper

1 Melt half the butter in a heavy pan, add the onion and garlic and cook for 10 minutes until softening. Add the chilli and cook for about 1 minute. Add the pumpkin or squash and cook, stirring constantly, for 5 minutes. Stir in the rosemary.

2 Add the rice and stir with a wooden spoon to coat with the oil and vegetables. Cook for 2–3 minutes to toast the rice grains.

3 Begin to add the stock, a large ladleful at a time, stirring all the time until each ladleful has been absorbed into the rice. The rice should always be bubbling slowly. If not, add some more stock. Continue adding the stock like this, until the rice is tender and creamy, but the grains remain firm, and the pumpkin is beginning to disintegrate. (This should take about 20 minutes, depending on the type of rice used.) Taste and season well with salt and pepper.

4 Stir the remaining butter and the cheese into the rice. Cover and allow to rest for 2–3 minutes, then serve straight away with extra Parmesan cheese.

This is more like a nutty pilaff than a classic risotto. Sweet leeks and roasted squash are superb with pearl barley, mushrooms and garlic.

BARLEY RISOTTO with ROASTED SQUASH

1 Rinse and drain the barley. Bring a pan of water to simmering point, add the barley and half-cover. Cook for 35–45 minutes, or until tender. Drain. Preheat the oven to 200°C|400°F|Gas 6.

2 Place the squash in a roasting pan with half the thyme. Season with pepper and toss with half the oil. Roast, stirring once, for 30–35 minutes, until tender and beginning to brown.

3 Heat half the butter with the remaining oil in a large frying pan. Cook the leeks and garlic gently for 5 minutes. Add the mushrooms and remaining thyme, then cook until the liquid from the mushrooms evaporates and the mushrooms begin to fry.

4 Stir in the carrots and cook for 2 minutes, then add the barley and most of the stock. Season and partially cover. Cook for 5 minutes. Pour in the remaining stock if necessary. Stir in the parsley, the remaining butter and half the Pecorino, then the squash, with salt and pepper to taste. Serve, sprinkled with pumpkin seeds and the remaining Pecorino.

INGREDIENTS
serves four to five

200g | 7oz | scant 1 cup pearl barley

1 butternut squash, peeled, seeded and cut into chunks

10ml | 2 tsp chopped fresh thyme

60ml | 4 tbsp olive oil

25g | 1oz | 2 tbsp butter

4 leeks, cut diagonally into fairly thick slices

2 garlic cloves, finely chopped

175g | 6oz | 2¼ cups chestnut mushrooms, sliced

2 carrots, coarsely grated

about 120ml | 4fl oz | ½ cup vegetable stock

30ml | 2 tbsp chopped fresh flat leaf parsley

50g | 2oz | ¼ cup Pecorino cheese, grated or shaved

45ml | 3 tbsp pumpkin seeds, toasted

salt and ground black pepper

You can serve this dish as a vegetarian meal on its own, as a side dish or as a topping for couscous. A dollop of garlic-flavoured yogurt or a spoonful of harissa goes very well with the squash and shallots. Try it with a green salad for supper.

BUTTERNUT SQUASH with PINK SHALLOTS

INGREDIENTS
serves four

900g | 2lb peeled butternut squash, cut into thick slices

120ml | 4fl oz | ½ cup water

45–60ml | 3–4 tbsp olive oil

knob (pat) of butter

16–20 pink shallots, peeled

10–12 garlic cloves, peeled

115g/ | 4oz | 1 cup blanched almonds

75g | 3oz | generous ½ cup raisins or sultanas (golden raisins), soaked in warm water for 15 minutes and drained

30–45ml | 2–3 tbsp clear honey

10ml | 2 tsp ground cinnamon

small bunch of mint, chopped

salt and ground black pepper

1 lemon, cut into wedges, to serve

1 Preheat the oven to 200°C | 400°F | Gas 6. Place the butternut squash in an ovenproof dish, add the water, cover and bake for about 45 minutes, until tender.

2 Meanwhile, heat the olive oil and butter in a large heavy pan. Stir in the shallots and cook until they begin to brown. Stir in the garlic and almonds.

3 When the garlic and almonds begin to brown, add the raisins or sultanas. Continue to cook until the shallots and garlic begin to caramelize, then stir in the honey and cinnamon, adding a little water if the mixture becomes too dry. Season well with salt and pepper and remove from the heat.

4 Cover the squash with the shallot and garlic mixture and return to the oven, uncovered, for a further 15 minutes. Sprinkle with fresh mint and serve with lemon wedges for squeezing over the vegetables.

COOK'S TIP When in season, substitute pumpkin for the squash.

Wild mushrooms combine especially well with eggs and spinach in this sensational soufflé. Almost any combination of mushrooms can be used for this recipe, although the firmer varieties provide the best texture.

SPINACH and WILD MUSHROOM SOUFFLÉ

INGREDIENTS
serves four

225g | 8oz fresh spinach, washed, or 115g | 4oz frozen chopped spinach

60ml | 4 tbsp unsalted (sweet) butter, plus extra for greasing

1 garlic clove, crushed

175g | 6oz | 1 3/4 cups assorted wild mushrooms such as ceps, bay boletes, saffron milk-caps, oyster, field mushrooms and hen of the woods, roughly chopped

250ml | 8fl oz | 1 cup milk

45ml | 3 tbsp plain (all-purpose) flour

6 eggs, separated

pinch grated nutmeg

175g | 6oz | 2 cups freshly grated Parmesan cheese

salt and ground black pepper

1 Preheat the oven to 190°C | 375°F | Gas 5. Steam the spinach over a moderate heat for 3–4 minutes. Cool under running water, then drain. Press out as much liquid as you can with the back of a large spoon and chop finely. If using frozen spinach, defrost and squeeze dry in the same way.

2 Gently sauté the garlic and mushrooms in the butter. Turn up the heat and evaporate the juices. When dry, add the spinach and transfer to a bowl. Cover and keep warm.

3 Measure 45ml | 3 tbsp of the milk into a bowl. Bring the remainder to a boil. Stir the flour and egg yolks into the milk in the bowl and blend well. Stir the boiling milk into the egg and flour mixture, return to the pan and simmer to thicken. Add the spinach mixture. Season to taste with salt, pepper and nutmeg.

4 Butter a 900ml | 1 1/2 pint | 3 3/4 cup soufflé dish, paying attention to the sides. Sprinkle with a little of the cheese. Set aside.

5 Whisk the egg whites until they hold soft peaks. Bring the spinach mixture back to a boil. Stir in a spoonful of beaten egg white, then fold the mixture into the remaining egg white. Turn into the soufflé dish, spread level, sprinkle with the remaining cheese and bake in the oven for about 25 minutes until puffed, risen and golden.

COOK'S TIP The soufflé dish can be prepared up to 12 hours in advance and reheated before the beaten egg whites are folded in.

In autumn, thoughts turn to hearty, satisfying food. This sustaining, yet low-fat dish is the ideal choice.

CASSEROLE with HARVEST VEGETABLES

1 Preheat the oven to 180°C | 350°F | Gas 4. Heat the oil in a large, flameproof casserole. Add the leeks, garlic and celery and cook over a low heat, stirring occasionally, for 3 minutes, until the leeks begin to soften.

2 Add the carrots, parsnips, sweet potato, swede, lentils, tomatoes, herbs and stock. Stir well and season with salt and pepper to taste. Bring to the boil, stirring occasionally.

3 Cover the casserole, put it in the oven and bake for about 50 minutes, until the vegetables and lentils are tender, stirring the vegetable mixture once or twice.

4 Remove the casserole from the oven. Blend the cornflour with the water in a small bowl. Stir the mixture into the casserole and heat it gently on top of the stove, stirring continuously, until the mixture boils and thickens. Lower the heat and simmer gently for 2 minutes, stirring.

5 Spoon on to warmed serving plates or into bowls, garnish with the thyme sprigs and serve.

INGREDIENTS
serves six

15ml | 1 tbsp sunflower oil

2 leeks, sliced

1 garlic clove, crushed

4 celery sticks, chopped

2 carrots, sliced

2 parsnips, diced

1 sweet potato, diced

225g | 8oz swede (rutabaga), diced

175g | 6oz | 3/4 cup whole brown or green lentils

450g | 1lb tomatoes, peeled, seeded and chopped

15ml | 1 tbsp chopped fresh thyme

15ml | 1 tbsp chopped fresh marjoram

900ml | 1 1/2 pints | 3 3/4 cups vegetable stock

15ml | 1 tbsp cornflour (cornstarch)

45ml | 3 tbsp water

salt and ground black pepper

fresh thyme sprigs, to garnish

The slightly smoky and earthy flavour of Jerusalem artichokes is excellent with shallots and smoked bacon. This dish makes a delicious accompaniment to chicken, roast cod or monkfish, or pork.

JERUSALEM ARTICHOKES with **BACON**

INGREDIENTS
serves four

50ml | 2fl oz | 1/4 cup butter

115g | 4oz smoked bacon or pancetta, chopped

800g | 1 3/4 lb Jerusalem artichokes, peeled

8–12 garlic cloves, peeled

115g | 4oz shallots, chopped

75ml | 5 tbsp water

30ml | 2 tbsp olive oil

120ml | 4fl oz | 1/2 cup fresh white breadcrumbs

30–45ml/2–3 tbsp chopped fresh parsley

salt and ground black pepper

1 Melt half the butter in a heavy frying pan and cook the chopped bacon or pancetta until brown and beginning to crisp. Remove half the bacon or pancetta from the pan and set aside.

2 Add the artichokes, garlic and shallots, and cook, stirring frequently, until the artichokes and garlic begin to brown slightly.

3 Season with salt and black pepper to taste and stir in the water. Cover and cook for another 8–10 minutes, shaking the pan occasionally.

4 Uncover the pan, increase the heat and cook for 5–6 minutes, until all the moisture has evaporated and the artichokes are tender.

5 In another frying pan, melt the remaining butter in the olive oil. Add the white breadcrumbs and fry over medium heat, stirring frequently, until crisp and golden. Stir in the chopped parsley and the reserved cooked bacon or pancetta.

6 Combine the artichokes with the breadcrumb mixture, mixing well. Adjust the seasoning if necessary, then turn into a warmed serving dish. Serve immediately.

COOK'S TIP Do not peel the artichokes too much in advance, as they discolour quickly on exposure to air. If necessary, drop them into a bowl of acidulated water. Alternatively, scrub them well and use with the skins still on.

There is nothing quite like the fragrance and flavour of rare Italian white truffles.

TAGLIARINI with WHITE TRUFFLE

INGREDIENTS
serves four

350g | 12oz fresh tagliarini

75g | 3oz | 6 tbsp butter, diced

60ml | 4 tbsp freshly grated Parmesan cheese

freshly grated nutmeg

1 small white truffle, about 25–40g | 1–1¹/₂oz

salt and ground black pepper

1 Bring a large pan of slightly salted water to the boil and cook the pasta until it is *al dente*. Immediately, drain it well and transfer it into a large, warmed bowl.

2 Add the diced butter, grated Parmesan and a little freshly grated nutmeg. Season with salt and pepper to taste. Toss well until all the strands are coated in melted butter.

3 Divide the pasta equally among four warmed, individual bowls and shave paper-thin slivers of the white truffle on top. Serve immediately.

COOK'S TIP It is worth tracking down fresh black or white truffles. Store fresh truffles at room temperature – keeping them with your eggs is a good way of sharing their musty aroma. Truffle shavings or truffle oil should only be added towards the end of cooking to preserve their full flavour.

VARIATION Since no one has managed to cultivate truffles, they remain rare and expensive. If you can't find the real thing try canned or bottled truffles. Preserved truffles are less flavoured and benefit from a drop or two of truffle oil. Never be tempted to add more than a few drops – if too much of this precious oil is used, it will impart a bitter taste.

This is a richly satisfying dish, combining sweet Spanish onions, pine nuts and Parmesan.

PASTA with SLOWLY COOKED ONIONS

1 Heat the butter and olive oil together in a large pan. Stir in the onions, cover and cook very gently, stirring occasionally, for about 20 minutes, until very soft.

2 Uncover and continue to cook gently until the onions have turned golden yellow. Add the balsamic vinegar and season well, then cook for another 1–2 minutes. Set aside.

3 Blanch the cavolo nero, spring greens, kale or Brussels sprout tops in boiling, lightly salted water for about 3 minutes. Drain well and add to the onions, then cook over low heat for 3–4 minutes.

4 Cook the pasta in boiling, lightly salted water for 8–12 minutes according to the package instructions, until just tender. Drain, then add to the pan of onions and greens and toss thoroughly to mix.

5 Season well with salt and pepper and stir in half the Parmesan. Transfer the pasta to warmed plates. Sprinkle the pine nuts and more Parmesan on top and serve immediately, offering more olive oil for drizzling on to taste.

VARIATION To make a delicious pilaff, cook 250g | 9oz | 1¼ cups brown basmati rice and use instead of the pasta.

INGREDIENTS
serves four

30ml | 2 tbsp butter

15ml1 tbsp extra virgin olive oil, plus more for drizzling (optional)

500g | 1¼lb Spanish (Bermuda) onions, halved and thinly sliced

5–10ml1–2 tsp balsamic vinegar

400–500g | 14oz–1¼lb cavolo nero, spring greens (collards), kale or Brussels sprout tops, shredded

400–500g | 14oz–1¼lb dried pasta (such as penne or fusilli)

75gl | 13oz | 1 cup freshly grated Parmesan cheese

120ml | 4fl oz | ½ cup pine nuts, toasted

salt and ground black pepper

Hot and Tasty

The onset of colder weather sharpens appetites for satisfying main courses. Try the ultimate fish pie, with a golden potato crust and chunks of cod and haddock, or mark the end of the barbecue season with fabulous hickory-smoked whole chicken with butternut pesto. Hearty stews are filling and delicious, and roasted meats and seasonal game birds make the perfect Sunday lunch.

The ultimate fish pie. Breaking through the golden potato crust reveals perfectly cooked chunks of cod and succulent tiger prawns swathed in a creamy parsley sauce. Cook in a big dish and bring triumphantly to the table.

FABULOUS FISH PIE with SAFFRON MASH

INGREDIENTS
serves six

750ml | 1¹/₄ pints | 3 cups milk

1 onion, chopped

1 bay leaf

2–3 peppercorns

450g | 1lb each of fresh cod fillet and smoked haddock fillet, skin on

350g | 12oz cooked tiger prawns (jumbo shrimp), shelled, with tails left on

75g | 3oz | 6 tbsp butter

75g | 3oz | ²/₃ cups plain (all-purpose) flour

60ml | 4 tbsp chopped fresh parsley

salt and ground black pepper

for the saffron mash

1.3kg | 3lb floury potatoes, peeled

large pinch saffron threads, soaked in 45ml | 3 tbsp hot water

75g | 3oz | 6 tbsp butter

250ml | 8fl oz | 1 cup milk

45ml | 3 tbsp chopped fresh dill, plus extra dill sprigs to garnish

1 Put the milk, onion, bay leaf and peppercorns into a large pan. Bring to the boil, then simmer for about 10 minutes. Set aside.

2 Lay the cod and haddock fillets, skin side up, in a roasting pan. Strain over the milk and simmer for 5–7 minutes on the hob (stovetop) until just opaque. Lift the fish out of the milk and transfer to a plate. Reserve the milk.

3 When the fish is cool enough to handle, pull off the skin and flake the flesh into large pieces, removing any bones. Transfer to a large bowl and add the shelled prawns.

4 Melt the butter in a small pan. Stir in the flour and cook for a minute or so, then gradually stir in the flavoured milk from the roasting pan until you achieve a smooth consistency. Whisk well and simmer gently for 15 minutes until thick and a little reduced, then taste and season with salt and pepper. Stir in the parsley.

5 Pour the sauce over the fish. Carefully mix together, transfer the mixture to a pie dish and leave to cool.

6 Preheat the oven to 180°C | 350°F | Gas 4. To make the saffron mash, boil the potatoes in salted water until tender, drain well and mash. Lump-free mashed potatoes are essential here; press them through a sieve to make sure they are really smooth. Using an electric whisk beat in the saffron and its soaking water, then the butter, milk and dill to make mashed potato that is light and fluffy. When the fish mixture has set, spoon over the golden mash, piling it on top. Bake for 30–40 minutes, or until the potato is golden brown and crisp. Serve immediately, garnished with dill.

Everything is cooked in one pot – the chunks of fresh, flaky cod, made yellow with saffron, are added at the last minute, and their flavour is offset by the smoked paprika-spiced beans. Serve with a big pile of crusty bread.

COD and **BEAN STEW** with **PAPRIKA**

1 Preheat the grill (broiler) and line the pan with foil. Halve the red pepper and scoop out the seeds. Place, cut side down, in the grill pan and grill (broil) under a high heat for about 10–15 minutes, until the skin is charred.

2 Put the pepper into a plastic bag, seal and leave for 10 minutes to steam. Remove from the bag, peel off the skin and discard. Chop the pepper into large pieces.

3 Roughly chop the bacon. Heat the olive oil in a pan, then add the bacon and garlic. Fry for 2 minutes, then add the sliced onion. Cover the pan and cook for about 5 minutes until the onion is soft. Stir in the paprika and pimentón, the saffron and its soaking water, and salt and pepper.

4 Stir the beans into the pan and add just enough stock to cover. Bring to the boil and simmer, uncovered, for about 15 minutes, stirring occasionally to prevent sticking. Stir in the chopped pepper and tomato quarters. Drop in the cubes of cod and bury them in the sauce. Cover and simmer for 5–7 minutes, or until cooked. Stir in the chopped coriander. Serve the stew in warmed soup plates or bowls, garnished with the coriander sprigs. Eat with lots of crusty bread.

INGREDIENTS
serves six to eight

1 large red (bell) pepper

45ml | 3 tbsp olive oil

4 rashers (strips) streaky (fatty) bacon

4 garlic cloves, finely chopped

1 onion, sliced

10ml | 2 tsp paprika

5ml | 1 tsp hot pimentón (smoked Spanish paprika)

large pinch of saffron threads soaked in 45ml | 3 tbsp hot water

400g | 14oz jar Spanish butter (lima) beans (judias del barco or judias blancas guisadas) or canned haricot (navy) beans, drained and rinsed

about 600ml | 1 pint | 2¹/₂ cups fish stock, or water and 60ml/4 tbsp Thai fish sauce

6 plum tomatoes, quartered

350g | 12oz fresh skinned cod fillet, cut into large chunks

salt and ground black pepper

45ml | 3 tbsp chopped fresh coriander (cilantro), plus a few sprigs to garnish

This traditional dish of fresh autumnal mussels cooked with shallots tastes as superb as it looks. Serve with crusty bread, or potatoes, to soak up the hot juices.

MUSSELS with SHALLOTS and SAFFRON

INGREDIENTS
serves six

2kg | 4¹/₂lb fresh mussels, scrubbed and beards removed

250g | 9oz shallots, finely chopped

300ml | ¹/₂ pint | 1¹/₄ cups medium white wine, such as Vouvray

generous pinch of saffron threads (about 12 threads)

75g | 3oz | 6 tbsp butter

2 celery sticks, finely chopped

5ml | 1 tsp fennel seeds, lightly crushed

2 large garlic cloves, finely chopped

250ml | 8fl oz | 1 cup fish or vegetable stock

1 bay leaf

pinch of cayenne pepper

2 large (US extra large) egg yolks

150ml | ¹/₄ pint | ²/₃ cup double (heavy) cream

juice of ¹/₂–1 lemon

30–45ml | 2–3 tbsp chopped fresh parsley

salt and ground black pepper

1 Discard any mussels that do not shut when tapped sharply.

2 Place 30ml | 2 tbsp of the shallots with the wine in a wide pan and bring to the boil. Add half the mussels and cover, then boil rapidly for 1 minute, shaking the pan once. Remove all the mussels, discarding any that remain closed. Repeat with the remaining mussels. Remove the top half-shell from each mussel. Strain the cooking liquid through a fine sieve into a bowl and stir in the saffron, then set aside.

3 Melt 50g | 2oz | ¹/₄ cup | 4 tbsp of the butter in a heavy pan. Add the remaining shallots and celery, and cook over a low heat, stirring occasionally, for 5–6 minutes, until softened but not browned. Add the fennel seeds and half of the garlic, then cook for another 2–3 minutes.

4 Pour in the reserved mussel liquid, bring to the boil and then simmer for 5 minutes before adding the stock, bay leaf and cayenne. Season with salt and pepper to taste, then simmer, uncovered, for 5–10 minutes.

5 Beat the egg yolks with the cream, then whisk in a ladleful of the hot liquid followed by the juice of ¹/₂ lemon. Whisk this mixture back into the sauce. Cook over a very low heat, without allowing it to boil, for 5–10 minutes, until slightly thickened. Taste for seasoning and add more lemon juice if necessary.

6 Stir the remaining garlic, butter and most of the parsley into the sauce with the mussels and reheat for 30–60 seconds. Distribute the mussels among six soup plates and ladle on the sauce. Sprinkle with the remaining parsley and serve.

Tart apples, plums and pears make a fabulous fruit stuffing that complements the rich gamey flavour of grouse perfectly. The rosy colour of the plums looks fantastic with the fresh green leaves of chard.

GROUSE with ORCHARD FRUITS

1 Sprinkle the lemon juice on the grouse and season it with salt and pepper. Melt half the butter in a flameproof casserole, add the grouse and cook for 10 minutes, until browned, turning occasionally. Use tongs to remove the grouse from the casserole and set aside.

2 Add the shallots to the fat remaining in the casserole and cook until softened but not coloured. Add the apple, pear, plums and allspice and cook for about 5 minutes, until the fruits are just beginning to soften. Remove the casserole from the heat and spoon the hot fruit mixture into the body cavities of the birds.

3 Truss the birds neatly with string. Smear the remaining butter on the birds and wrap them in the chard leaves, then replace them in the casserole.

4 Pour in the Marsala and heat until simmering. Cover tightly and simmer for 20 minutes, until the birds are tender, taking care not to overcook them. Let rest in a warm place for about 10 minutes before serving.

COOK'S TIP There isn't a lot of liquid in the casserole for cooking the birds – they are steamed rather than boiled – so it is very important that the casserole is heavy with a tight-fitting lid, otherwise the liquid may evaporate and the chard burn on the bottom of the pan.

INGREDIENTS
serves two

juice of 1/2 lemon

2 young grouse

50ml | 2fl oz | 1/4 cup butter

4 Swiss chard leaves

50ml | 2fl oz | 1/4 cup Marsala

salt and ground black pepper

for the stuffing

2 shallots, finely chopped

1 apple, peeled, cored and chopped

1 pear, peeled, cored and chopped

2 plums, halved, stoned (pitted) and chopped

large pinch of allspice

Whole chicken smoked over hickory wood chips acquires a perfectly tanned skin and succulent pinkish flesh. The butternut squash roasts alongside it wrapped in foil, and is later transformed into a delicious pesto. The chicken also tastes great cold so, if your barbecue is large enough, try smoking two at once, for a delicious meal the next day.

SMOKED CHICKEN with BUTTERNUT PESTO

INGREDIENTS
serves four to six

roasting chicken, about 1.3kg | 3lb

1 lemon, quartered

8–10 fresh bay leaves

3 branches fresh rosemary

15ml | 1 tbsp olive oil

salt and ground black pepper

kitchen string (twine)

4 handfuls hickory wood chips soaked in cold water for at least 30 minutes

for the pesto

1 butternut squash, about 675g | 1¹/₂lb, halved and seeded

2 garlic cloves, sliced

2 fresh thyme sprigs

45ml | 3 tbsp olive oil

25g | 1oz | ¹/₃ cup freshly grated Parmesan cheese

1 Prepare the barbecue. Season the inside of the chicken and stuff with lemon quarters, bay leaves and sprigs from one rosemary branch. Tie the legs together with kitchen string and rub the bird all over with the oil. Season the skin lightly.

2 To prepare the butternut squash for the pesto cut it into eight pieces and lay them on a piece of double foil. Season well and sprinkle with the garlic and thyme leaves. Drizzle over 15ml | 1 tbsp of the olive oil and a sprinkling of water. Bring the sides of the foil up to completely enclose the squash and secure the parcel.

3 Once the flames have died down, rake the hot coals to one side and insert a drip tray filled with water beside them. Position an oiled grill rack over the coals to heat. When the coals are hot, or covered with a light coating of ash, place the chicken on the grill rack above the drip tray, with the squash next to it, over the coals. Cover the barbecue with a lid or tented heavy-duty foil. Cook the squash for 35 minutes, or until tender.

4 Drain the hickory chips, carefully add a handful to the coals and replace the lid. Cook the chicken for 1–1¹/₄ hours more, adding a handful of hickory chips every 15 minutes. Add the remaining rosemary to the coals with the last batch of hickory chips. When the chicken is done, transfer it to a plate, cover with tented foil and leave to stand for 10 minutes.

5 Unwrap the butternut squash. Leaving the thyme stalk behind, scoop the flesh and the garlic into a food processor. Pulse until the mixture forms a thick purée. Add the Parmesan, and then the remaining oil, pulsing to ensure it is well combined. Spoon into a bowl and serve with the hot chicken.

Earthy and substantial, this is the ideal dish for chilly autumn evenings. The beans acquire layers of taste when slow-cooked in the rich sauce provided by the meat.

LAMB SHANKS with CANNELLINI BEANS

INGREDIENTS
serves four

4 lamb shanks

45ml | 3 tbsp plain (all-purpose) flour

45ml | 3 tbsp extra virgin olive oil

1 large onion, chopped

2 garlic cloves, sliced

1 celery stick, sliced

1 carrot, sliced

leaves from 2 fresh rosemary sprigs

2 bay leaves

175ml | 6fl oz | 3/4 cup white wine

30ml | 2 tbsp tomato purée (paste)

225g | 8oz | 1 cup dried cannellini beans, soaked overnight in water to cover

150ml | 1/4 pint | 2/3 cups hot water

salt and ground black pepper

1 Preheat the oven to 160°C | 325°F | Gas 3. Season the lamb shanks and coat them lightly in flour. Heat the oil in a large flameproof casserole over a high heat and brown the pieces of meat on all sides. Lift them out and set them aside.

2 Add the onion to the oil remaining in the casserole and sauté gently. As soon as it is light golden, stir in the garlic, celery, carrot, rosemary and bay leaves.

3 Put the meat back in the pan and pour the wine slowly over it. Let it bubble and reduce, then stir in the tomato purée diluted in about 450ml | 3/4 pint | scant 2 cups of hot water. Drain the soaked beans and add them to the pan with black pepper to taste. Mix well. Cover the casserole, transfer it to the oven and bake for 1 hour. Stir in salt to taste and add the hot water. Cover and cook for 1 hour more, or until tender.

Roasts make great Sunday lunches because they require minimum attention once they are in the oven, so the cook can relax with the family or friends.

STUFFED LOIN of PORK with APPLE SAUCE

1 Preheat the oven to 220°C | 425°F | Gas 7. Heat the oil in a large pan and cook the leeks until softened. Stir in the apricots, dates, breadcrumbs, eggs and thyme, and season with salt and pepper.

2 Lay the pork skin side up and use a sharp knife to score the rind crossways. Turn the meat over and cut down the centre of the joint to within 1cm | ½in of the rind and fat, then work from the middle outwards towards one side, cutting most of the meat off the rind, keeping a 1cm | ½in layer of meat on top of the rind. Cut to within 2.5cm | 1in of the side of the joint. Repeat on the other side of the joint.

3 Spoon half the stuffing over the joint, then fold the meat over it. Tie the joint back into its original shape, then place in a roasting tin and rub the skin liberally with salt. Roast for 40 minutes, then reduce the oven temperature to 190°C | 375C°F | Gas 5 and cook for a further 1½ hours, or until the meat is tender and cooked through. When cooked, cover the meat closely with foil and leave to stand in a warm place for 10 minutes before carving.

4 Meanwhile, shape the remaining stuffing into walnut-sized balls. Arrange on a tray, cover with clear film and chill until 20 minutes before the pork is cooked. Then add the stuffing balls to the roasting tin and baste them with the cooking juices from the meat.

5 To make the apple sauce, peel, core and chop the apples, then place them in a small pan with the cider or water and cook for 5–10 minutes, stirring occasionally, or until very soft. Beat well or process in a blender to make smooth apple sauce. Beat in the butter and sugar, adding a little more sugar to taste, if required.

INGREDIENTS
serves six

15ml | 1 tbsp light olive oil

2 leeks, chopped

150g | 5oz | ⅔ cup ready-to-eat dried apricots, chopped

150g | 5oz | 1 cup dried dates, stoned (pitted) and chopped

75g | 3oz | 1½ cups fresh white breadcrumbs

2 eggs, beaten

15ml | 1 tbsp fresh thyme leaves

1.5kg | 3⅓lb boned loin of pork

salt and ground black pepper

for the apple sauce

450g | 1lb cooking apples

30ml | 2 tbsp dry (hard) cider or water

25g | 1oz | 2 tbsp butter

about 25g | 1oz | 2 tbsp caster (superfine) sugar

This hearty stew is both tasty and colourful. The combination of the spicy meat and sweet peppers is sure to warm you as the autumn winds begin to blow outside. Serve with plenty of mashed potato.

SPICY SAUSAGE and PEPPER STEW

1 Halve and seed the peppers and cut them into quarters. Heat the olive oil in a large heavy pan, add the peppers and sauté them over a medium heat for 10–15 minutes until they start to brown.

2 Meanwhile, slice the sausages into bitesize chunks. Carefully tip the hot olive oil into a frying pan. Add the sausages and fry them briefly, turning them frequently, to get rid of the excess fat but not to cook them. As soon as they are brown, remove the sausages from the pan with a slotted spoon and drain them on a plate lined with kitchen paper.

3 Add the tomatoes, sausages and herbs to the peppers. Stir in the water and season with salt and pepper, then cover the pan and cook gently for about 30 minutes. Mix in the parsley and serve.

VARIATION If you prefer, you can stir in the parsley, spread the mixture in a medium baking dish and bake it in an oven preheated to 180°C│350°F│Gas 4. Cook for about 40 minutes, stirring occasionally and adding more hot water when needed.

COOK'S TIP The peppers used in this recipe are the elongated, sweet yellow and green ones. However, you can also use elongated red peppers or a mixture of the bell-shaped red, green and yellow peppers that are more commonly found.

INGREDIENTS
serves four

675g │ 1¹/₂lb sweet peppers

75ml │ 5 tbsp extra virgin olive oil

500g │ 1¹/₄lb spicy sausages (Italian garlic sausages, Merguez or Toulouse)

400g │ 14oz tomatoes, roughly sliced

5ml │ 1 tsp dried oregano or some fresh thyme, chopped

150ml │ ¹/₄ pint │ ²/₃ cup hot water

45ml │ 3 tbsp chopped flat leaf parsley

salt and ground black pepper

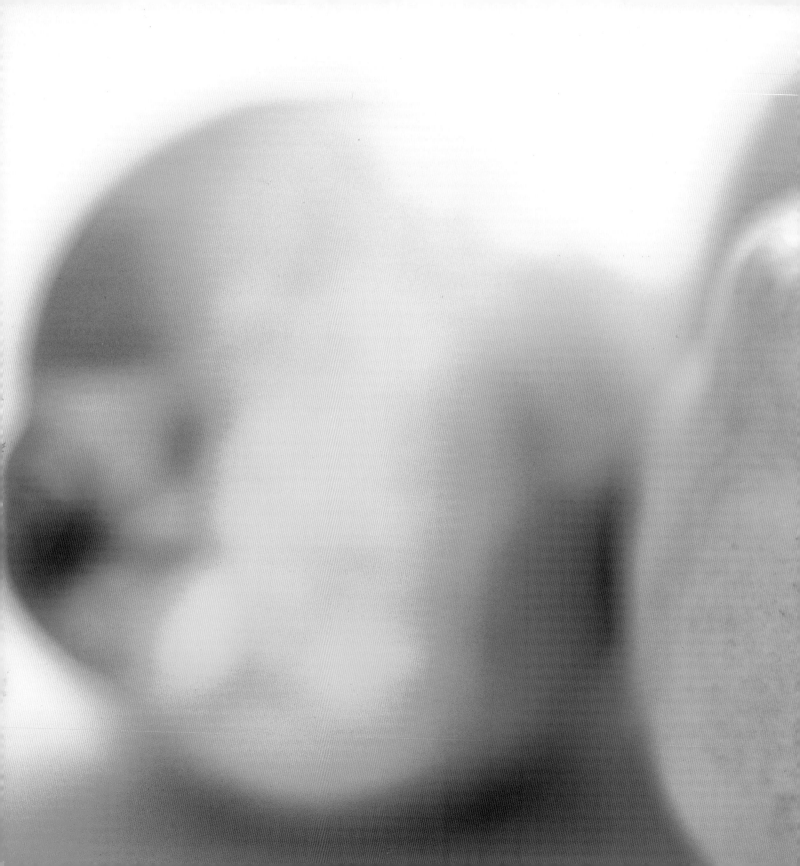

Abundant and Fruity

Autumn's generous harvest of fruit and nuts from the woods and hedgerows provides the basis for jellies and chutneys, as well as for intensely flavoured desserts. Enjoy the traditional combination of blackberry and apple in a hot pudding, or crisp fresh hazelnuts in a mouthwatering tart, and mark a special occasion with an indulgent dessert of pears flavoured with cloves, coffee and maple syrup.

If you use eating apples bursting with flavour, loads of butter and sugar and make your own shortcrust pastry, then an apple pie can't go wrong. However, adding a buttery caramel to the apples takes it one step further and, coupled with the mixed spice, gives a rich flavour to the juices in the pie.

DEEP DISH APPLE PIE

INGREDIENTS
serves six

900g | 2lb eating apples

75g | 3oz | 6 tbsp unsalted (sweet) butter

45–60ml | 3–4 tbsp demerara (raw) sugar

3 cloves

2.5ml | ½ tsp mixed (apple pie) spice

clotted cream, ice cream or double (heavy) cream, to serve

for the pastry

250g | 9oz | 2¼ cups plain (all-purpose) flour

pinch of salt

50g | 2oz | ¼ cup lard or white cooking fat, chilled and diced

75g | 3oz | 6 tbsp unsalted (sweet) butter, chilled and diced

30–45ml | 2–3 tbsp chilled water

a little milk, for brushing

caster (superfine) sugar, for dredging

1 Preheat the oven to 200°C | 400°F | Gas 6. Make the pastry first. Sift together the flour and salt into a bowl. Rub in the lard or fat and butter until the mixture resembles fine breadcrumbs. Stir in enough chilled water to bring the pastry together. Knead lightly, then wrap in clear film (plastic wrap) and chill for 30 minutes.

2 To make the filling, peel, core and thickly slice the apples. Melt the butter in a frying pan, add the sugar and cook for 3–4 minutes, allowing it to melt and caramelize. Add the apples and stir around to coat. Cook over a brisk heat until the apples take on a little colour, add the spices and tip out into a bowl to cool slightly.

3 Divide the pastry in two and, on a lightly floured surface, roll out into two rounds that will easily fit a deep 23cm | 9in pie plate. Line the plate with one round of pastry. Spoon in the cooled filling and mound up in the centre. Cover the apples with the remaining pastry, sealing and crimping the edges. Make a 5cm | 2in long slit through the top of the pastry to allow the steam to escape. Brush the pie with milk and dredge with caster sugar.

4 Place the pie on a baking sheet and bake in the oven for 25–35 minutes until golden and firm. Serve with clotted cream, ice cream or double cream.

This perennial favourite is a great way to take advantage of the season's apple harvest. There are any number of local apple varieties, so this cake will always be unique.

COUNTRY APPLE CAKE

INGREDIENTS
makes one 18cm/7in cake

115g | 4oz | ½ cup soft non-hydrogenated margarine

115g | 4oz | ½ cup unrefined soft light brown sugar or rapadura

2 eggs, beaten

115g | 4oz | 1 cup self-raising (self-rising) flour, sifted

50g | 2oz | ½ cup rice flour

5ml | 1 tsp baking powder

10ml | 2 tsp mixed (apple pie) spice

1 cooking apple, cored and chopped

115g | 4oz | scant 1 cup raisins

about 60ml | 4 tbsp milk or soya milk

15g | 2 tbsp flaked (sliced) almonds

1 Preheat the oven to 160°C | 325°F | Gas 3. Lightly grease and line a deep 18cm | 7in round, loose-bottomed cake tin (pan).

2 Cream the margarine and sugar in a mixing bowl. Gradually add the eggs, then fold in the flours, baking powder and spice.

3 Stir in the chopped apple, raisins and enough of the milk to make a soft, dropping consistency.

4 Turn the mixture into the prepared tin and level the surface. Sprinkle the flaked almonds over the top. Bake the cake for 1–1¼ hours until risen, firm to the touch and golden brown.

5 Cool the apple cake in the tin for about 10 minutes, then turn out onto a wire rack to cool. Cut into slices when cold. Alternatively, serve the cake warm, in slices, with custard or ice cream. Store the cold cake in an airtight container or wrapped in foil.

VARIATIONS
• Use sultanas (golden raisins) or chopped dried apricots or pears instead of the raisins.
• A wide variety of organic ice creams is available from independent dairies and supermarkets – vanilla goes particularly well with this cake.

Pears are at their best in autumn and, combined with other ingredients such as cloves, coffee and maple syrup, they form the basis of this indulgent dessert.

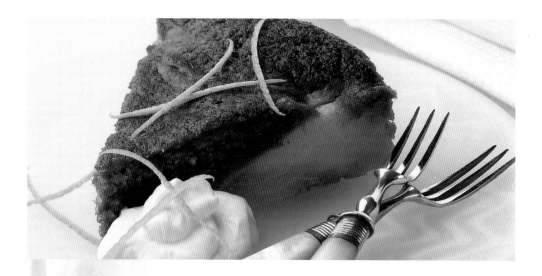

STICKY PEAR PUDDING with ORANGE CREAM

1 Preheat the oven to 180°C|350°F|Gas 4. Lightly grease a 20cm|8in loose-based sandwich tin (shallow cake pan). Put the ground coffee in a bowl and pour 15ml|1 tbsp of boiling water over. Leave to infuse for 4 minutes, then strain through a fine sieve.

2 Peel, halve and core the pears. Thinly slice across the pear halves part of the way through. Brush the pears with orange juice. Grind the hazelnuts in a coffee grinder until fine. Beat the butter and the caster sugar together until very light and fluffy. Gradually beat in the eggs, then fold in the flour, ground cloves, hazelnuts and coffee. Spoon the mixture into the prepared sandwich tin and level the surface with a spatula.

3 Pat the pears dry on kitchen paper, then arrange them carefully in the sponge mixture, flat side down. Lightly press two whole cloves, if using, into each pear half. Brush the pears with 15ml|1 tbsp maple syrup. Sprinkle 15ml|1 tbsp caster sugar over the pears. Bake for 45–50 minutes, or until firm and well risen.

4 While the sponge is cooking, make the orange cream. Whip the cream, icing sugar and orange rind until soft peaks form. Spoon into a serving dish and chill until needed.

5 Allow the sponge to cool for about 10 minutes in the tin, then remove and place on a serving plate. Lightly brush with the remaining maple syrup before decorating with orange rind and serving warm with the orange cream.

COOK'S TIP
Buy slightly under-ripe pears and leave them to ripen on a sunny windowsill for a few days – over-ripe pears go off quickly.

INGREDIENTS
serves six

30ml|2 tbsp ground coffee

4 ripe pears

juice of 1/2 orange

50g|2oz|1/2 cup toasted hazelnuts

115g|4oz|1/2 cup butter, softened

115g|4oz|generous 1/2 cup unrefined caster (superfine) sugar or rapadura, plus an extra 15ml|1 tbsp for baking

2 eggs, beaten

50g|2oz|1/2 cup self-raising (self-rising) flour, sifted

pinch of ground cloves

16 whole cloves (optional)

45ml|3 tbsp maple syrup

fine strips of orange rind, to decorate

for the orange cream
300ml|1/2 pint|1 1/4 cups whipping cream

15ml|1 tbsp unrefined icing (confectioner's) sugar, sifted

finely grated rind of 1/2 orange

The deliciously tart autumn flavours of blackberry and apple complement each other perfectly to make a light and mouthwatering hot pudding.

HOT BLACKBERRY and APPLE SOUFFLÉS

1 Preheat the oven to 200°C | 400°F | Gas 6. Generously grease six 150ml | 1/4 pint | 2/3 cup individual soufflé dishes with butter, and dust with caster sugar, shaking out the excess.

2 Put a baking sheet in the oven to heat. Cook the blackberries, diced apple and orange rind and juice in a pan for about 10 minutes or until the apple has pulped down well. Press through a sieve into a bowl. Stir in 50g | 2oz | 1/4 cup of the caster sugar. Set aside to cool.

3 Put a spoonful of the fruit purée into each prepared soufflé dish and spread evenly. Set the dishes aside.

4 Place the egg whites in a grease-free bowl and whisk until they form stiff peaks. Very gradually whisk in the remaining caster sugar to make a stiff, glossy meringue mixture.

5 Fold in the remaining fruit purée and spoon the flavoured meringue into the prepared dishes. Level the tops with a palette knife (metal spatula), and run a table knife around the inside edge of each dish.

6 Place the dishes on the hot baking sheet and bake for 10–15 minutes until the soufflés have risen well and are lightly browned. Dust the tops with icing sugar and serve immediately.

COOK'S TIP Running a table knife around the inside edge of the soufflé dishes before baking helps the soufflés to rise evenly without sticking to the rim of the dish.

INGREDIENTS
serves six

butter or non-hydrogenated margarine, for greasing

150g | 5oz | 3/4 cup unrefined caster (superfine) sugar or rapadura, plus extra for dusting

350g | 12oz | 3 cups blackberries

1 large cooking apple, peeled and finely diced

grated rind and juice of 1 orange

3 egg whites

unrefined icing (confectioner's) sugar, for dusting

The honey-soft texture and the richness of the walnuts make this cake irresistible.

MOIST WALNUT CAKE with BRANDY

INGREDIENTS
serves ten to twelve

150g | 5oz | 2/3 cup unsalted (sweet) butter

115g | 4oz | generous 1/2 cup caster (superfine) sugar

4 eggs, separated

60ml | 4 tbsp brandy

2.5ml | 1/2 tsp ground cinnamon

300g | 11oz | 2 3/4 cups shelled walnuts

150g | 5oz | 1 1/4 cups self-raising (self-rising) flour

5ml | 1 tsp baking powder

salt

for the syrup

250g | 9oz | generous 1 cup caster (superfine) sugar

30ml | 2 tbsp brandy

2–3 strips of pared orange rind

2 cinnamon sticks

1 Preheat the oven to 190°C | 375°F | Gas 5. Grease a 35 x 23cm | 14 x 9in roasting pan or baking dish that is at least 5cm/2in deep. Cream the butter in a large mixing bowl until soft, then add the sugar and beat well until the mixture is light and fluffy. Add the egg yolks one by one, beating the mixture after each addition. Stir in the brandy and cinnamon. Coarsely chop the walnuts in a food processor, then stir them into the mixture using a wooden spoon. Do not use an electric mixer at this stage.

2 Sift the flour with the baking powder and set aside. Whisk the egg whites with a pinch of salt until they are stiff. Fold them into the creamed mixture, alternating with tablespoons of flour until the egg whites and the flour have all been incorporated.

3 Spread the mixture evenly in the prepared pan or dish. It should be about 4cm | 1 1/2in deep. Bake for about 40 minutes, until the top is golden and a skewer inserted in the cake comes out clean. Take the cake out of the oven and let it rest in the pan or dish while you make the syrup.

4 Mix the sugar and 300ml | 1/2 pint | 1 1/4 cups water in a small pan. Heat gently, stirring, until the sugar has dissolved. Bring to the boil, lower the heat and add the brandy, orange rind and cinnamon sticks. Simmer for 10 minutes. Slice the cake into 6cm | 2 1/2in diamond or square shapes while still hot and strain the syrup slowly over it. Let it stand for 10–20 minutes until it has absorbed the syrup and is thoroughly soaked.

COOK'S TIP The cake will stay moist for 2–3 days, and tastes even better the day after it has been made, provided it is covered with clear film (plastic wrap), and does not need to go into the refrigerator. Serve it with coffee or a glass of brandy.

Dark muscovado sugar gives this dessert its deliciously smooth butterscotch flavour.

BUTTERSCOTCH and HAZELNUT TART

1 Break up the biscuits slightly, put them in a strong plastic bag and crush them with a rolling pin. Tip them into a bowl and add the toasted nuts and the butter. Mix until evenly combined.

2 Press on to the bottom and slightly up the sides of a 24cm|9½in loose-based flan tin or freezer-proof pie dish that is about 4cm|1½in deep.

3 Whisk the evaporated milk and sugar in a large bowl until the mixture is pale and thick and leaves a thick trail when the whisk is lifted.

4 In a separate grease-free bowl, whisk the egg white until stiff. Whip the double cream separately until it forms soft peaks.

5 Using a large metal spoon, fold first the cream and then the egg white into the whisked evaporated milk and sugar. Pour the mixture into the biscuit case. Cover and freeze overnight.

6 To serve, sprinkle the tart with hazelnuts and demerara sugar and cut into wedges.

COOK'S TIPS
• Remember to chill the evaporated milk for a couple of hours before you are ready to make the filling. This will ensure that it whisks well.
• Ground and chopped pecans, walnuts and almonds can be used instead of the hazelnuts.

INGREDIENTS
serves eight

for the case

90g|3½oz gingernut biscuits (gingersnaps)

75g|3oz|¼ cup ground hazelnuts, toasted

50g|2oz|¼ cup unsalted (sweet) butter, melted

for the filling

300ml|½ pint|1¼ cups evaporated (unsweetened condensed) milk, chilled

150g|5oz|⅔ cup dark muscovado sugar

1 egg white

150ml|¼ pint|⅔ cup double (heavy) cream

chopped toasted hazelnuts and demerara (raw) sugar, to decorate

These luscious pastries use the season's plum harvest to great effect. The minute they have cooled down, they are sure to be snapped up quickly.

PLUM and MARZIPAN PASTRIES

INGREDIENTS
serves six

375g | 13oz ready-rolled puff pastry

90ml | 6 tbsp plum jam

115g | 4oz | 1/2 cup white marzipan, coarsely grated

3 red plums

1 egg, beaten

50g | 2oz | 1/2 cup flaked (sliced) almonds

for the glaze

30ml | 2 tbsp plum jam

15ml | 1 tbsp water

1 Preheat the oven to 220°C | 425°F | Gas 7. Unroll the pastry, cut it into six equal squares and then place on one or two dampened baking sheets.

2 Halve and stone (pit) the red plums. Using a small spoon, place 15ml | 1 tbsp plum jam into the centre of each puff pastry square, leaving a border all around. Divide the marzipan among them. Place half a plum, hollow side down, on top of each mound of marzipan.

3 Brush the edges of the pastry with a little beaten egg. Bring up the corners of the pastry and lightly press the edges together, then open out the corners at the top. Glaze the pastries with some more beaten egg, then press a sixth of the flaked almonds on each.

4 Bake the pastries for 20–25 minutes, or until lightly golden.

5 Meanwhile, to make the glaze, heat the jam and water in a pan, stirring until smooth. Press the mixture through a sieve into a bowl, then lightly brush it over the tops of the pastries while they are still warm. Leave the pastries to cool on a wire rack before serving at room temperature.

COOK'S TIP Ready-rolled puff pastry has been used here for speed and convenience. If you make your own, the squares should measure 15cm | 6in.

Quinces are less common than they once were, perhaps because they are not good to eat raw, but they are not difficult to grow, and well worth it for their wonderfully rich, fragrant flavour when cooked – here enhanced by the fresh rosemary.

QUINCE and ROSEMARY JELLY

INGREDIENTS
makes about 900g | 2lb

900g | 2lb quinces

900ml | 1½ pints | 3¾ cups water

4 large sprigs of fresh rosemary

preserving or granulated sugar

1 Cut the quinces into small pieces, discarding any bruised parts. Put them in a large heavy pan with the water (see Cook's Tip).

2 Reserve a few small sprigs of rosemary, then add the rest to the pan. Bring to the boil, then reduce the heat, cover and simmer gently until the fruit is very soft and pulpy.

3 Remove and discard the rosemary sprigs (it doesn't matter if the leaves have fallen off). Pour the fruit and juice into a sterilized jelly bag suspended over a large bowl. Leave for 3 hours, or until it stops dripping.

4 Measure the juice into the cleaned pan and add 450g | 1lb | 2¼ cups sugar for every 600ml | 1 pint | 2½ cups juice. Heat gently, stirring occasionally until the sugar has dissolved. Bring to the boil, then boil rapidly for about 10 minutes. When the jelly reaches setting point, remove the pan from the heat.

5 Skim the surface using a slotted spoon to remove any froth. Leave to cool for a few minutes until a thin skin forms on the surface. Place a sprig of fresh rosemary in each warmed sterilized jar, then pour in the jelly. Cover and seal immediately. Store the jelly in a cool, dark place and use within a year of making. Once opened, keep in the refrigerator and eat within 3 months.

COOK'S TIP The amount of water needed for this jelly varies according to the ripeness of the fruit. For a good set, hard, under-ripe quinces should be used; if the fruit is soft, you will need to add a little lemon juice and less water.

This is a classic chutney to make when the last tomatoes have refused to ripen. Preparing your own pickling spice makes it easy to add exactly the right amount of flavour.

GREEN TOMATO CHUTNEY

1 Place the tomatoes, apples, onions and garlic in a large pan. Add the salt. Tie the pickling spice in a piece of muslin (cheesecloth) and add to the pan.

2 Add half the vinegar to the pan and bring to the boil. Reduce the heat and simmer for 1 hour, or until the chutney is thick, stirring frequently.

3 Dissolve the sugar in the remaining vinegar and add to the chutney. Simmer for 1 1/2 hours until the chutney is thick, stirring occasionally. Remove the muslin bag from the chutney. Spoon the hot chutney into warmed sterilized jars. Cover with airtight, vinegar-proof lids and store for at least one month before using.

COOK'S TIP To avoid spillages, use a jam funnel to transfer the chutney into the jars. Wipe the jars and label them when cold.

INGREDIENTS
makes about 2.5kg | 5 1/2lb

1.75kg | 3 3/4lb green tomatoes, roughly chopped

450g | 1lb cooking apples, peeled, cored and chopped

450g | 1lb onions, chopped

2 large garlic cloves, crushed

15ml | 1 tbsp salt

45ml | 3 tbsp pickling spice

600ml | 1 pint | 2 1/2 cups cider vinegar

450g | 1lb | 2 cups granulated sugar

Winter Cooking

INTRODUCTION

Winter is the season for inner warmth, when sharing good things brings a positive glow of goodwill to dull days. Traditions focus on entertaining at home, sharing simple, warming suppers and gathering for Saturday dinner or Sunday lunch. Everyday meals are generally more substantial than at other times of the year.

This is the season to indulge in comforting nursery foods, but these days there is also an urge to balance them with lighter dishes with a modern twist. While the weather is cold and crisp, hot and healthy meals fuel invigorating walks and energetic snow sports. When spirits flag, steaming hot broth, healing drinks and tempting toddies are soothing restoratives.

Winter goodness

While global distribution systems mean that virtually all ingredients are obtainable throughout the year, concentrating on food from close to home is the way to eat affordable, good-quality meals with maximum food value. Focusing on seasonal produce is sensible for a healthy diet because the type of foods that nature makes available complement the body's needs. As the weather becomes cold, energy-giving foods and ingredients for hot dishes are more plentiful.

FISH AND SEAFOOD

Supplies of some fresh fish and seafood can be unreliable when fleets cannot venture into rough seas. Oysters and mussels are good winter shellfish. Smoked fish, such as trout, mackerel and kippers are versatile, and preserved herrings (pickled in vinegar or salted and packed in oil) are a good store-cupboard standby for supper dishes or appetizers. Fresh fish such as red mullet and turbot are also available in the winter months.

MEAT, POULTRY AND GAME

Goose is the seasonal poultry to enjoy during winter months; its dark flesh complemented by rich wine gravies and tangy fruit sauces. Fresh whole turkey is a favourite choice for celebrations. Guinea fowl (now farmed) is a tasty alternative to chicken for roasting, and mature pheasants make excellent casseroles.

Seasons for wild deer overlap, and farmed venison is always available, but winter is when this rich, dark meat is really popular. Large roasts taken from the haunch are very grand; succulent casseroles, and steaks braised in rich sauces are particularly good for winter dinner parties. Baked ham or gammon on the bone is commonly served as the centrepiece of a cold buffet but is also good hot. Beef and pork are also popular for casseroles and stews.

Full-flavoured casseroles, meat sauces, sausages and pâtés using liver, kidneys and other types of offal are welcome for everyday meals. Scottish haggis (a spicy sausage made with offal and oats) is good with a rich whisky sauce. Grilled or pan-fried kidneys are a special choice for leisurely weekend breakfasts, especially with bacon, eggs, hash browns or rösti, succulent sausages and mushrooms.

VERSATILE VEGETABLES

Roots and tubers are satisfying and versatile ingredients in winter cooking. Large fluffy potatoes bake well and make excellent hot-pot toppings and roast wedges. Jerusalem artichokes, parsnips and swedes are on top form. Pass on frilly greens and opt for flavoursome winter cabbage, kale and Brussels sprouts. Sprouted beans and seeds are delicious in stir-fries or salads and are an excellent source of vitamin C. Chestnuts can be roasted as a snack or boiled, peeled and used as a vegetable. They are delicious hot with winter greens and zesty orange or combined with dried fruit in stuffings or pilaff.

WINTER FRUIT

The citrus season in January and February brings Seville or Bigarade oranges that are used for that essentially British preserve, marmalade. These bitter fruits also make full-flavoured savoury sauces and relishes, such as Bigarade sauce to go with roast duck. Tangerines, including mandarins, clementines and satsumas, are juicy and full of flavour, as are seedless navel or navelina oranges. Catch fresh cranberries while they are available, and make the most of pomegranates and pineapples, which are good in early winter. Bananas, apples and kiwi fruit are good everyday snacks or dessert ingredients, with exotic fruit providing extra variety when it is available.

Dried fruit and nuts are harvested and dried in the late autumn and winter months. Good in both savoury and dessert recipes, they are often associated with seasonal celebrations. Apricots, peaches, prunes, dates and figs make excellent compotes and are deliciously warming in pies, crumbles and other winter puddings.

Hot tips for a winter chill

Covered markets are vibrant areas in towns and cities and ideal for relaxed winter shopping. They provide a colourful backdrop for butchers, bakers and the smallest of local producers. Shop early in the day, because local cheeses, the best offers from butchers and the most popular home-baked breads, pies and cakes sell quickly.

Small to medium producers of seasonal specialities and high-quality ingredients, such as poultry, meat, game, cheese, confectionery and premium preserves, offer mail-order services, or home delivery through internet ordering. This is particularly useful for foods that have to be ordered in advance anyway, such as fresh goose or turkey, or large cuts of meat.

FUSS-FREE SIMMERING

It is a myth that many long-cooked classic dishes are demanding. With a little forethought, the ingredients can be put to simmer and left virtually unattended for anything from 1 to 4 hours. Softening or browning onions, vegetables and meat first is necessary for sauces and moist dishes that are cooked for about an hour. For incredible depth of flavour, invest in a big ovenproof cooking pot with a close-fitting lid. Simply mix or layer all the ingredients in the pot with herbs and seasoning. Bring the liquid (water, stock or wine) to the boil before pouring it into the pot. Cover closely and cook until the liquid is just about to boil, then continue to cook gently in the oven or on top of the stove for 2 to 4 hours, depending on the ingredients. Casseroles with meat or dried beans can be cooked for up to 5 hours for rich and succulent results.

- Raw spices, such as whole, crushed or ground coriander and whole or ground cumin, should be cooked briefly in a little oil or butter before they are simmered, as they can taste slightly harsh, particularly when used in significant quantities.

- Herbs and spices with warm flavours are ideal for winter stews and sauces. Rosemary, bay and marjoram; juniper, cinnamon, nutmeg and mace are excellent winter aromatics. Juniper is a favourite for venison, and beef or pork stews with a gamey flavour.

- Bake little rounds of bread spread with butter and mustard until crisp and golden, then serve as a topping for juicy dishes to add contrasting texture.

- Add canned beans to long-cooked stews to turn them into satisfying one-pot meals. Borlotti, cannellini, flageolet and kidney beans or chickpeas are delicious with rich sauces. It's best to rinse them first, as they can be salty.

- Stir-fried greens are a quick and easy accompaniment to long-cooked casseroles. Shred kale or cabbage and stir-fry briefly with a sprinkling of caraway or fennel seeds.

Restorative recipes

On a cold day, there's nothing like a pot of broth to fill the senses and satisfy the appetite. Just one steaming bowlful brings an inimitable sense of wellbeing. Chicken and beef make fabulous broth; the secret lies in selecting cuts on the bone, roasting very briefly at a high temperature until brown for a rich flavour, then simmering gently with large chunks of onion, carrot, celery, a long twist of lemon rind and several bay leaves. Once strained, the meat should be diced, and lots of diced or shredded vegetables added to the broth and cooked gently. Served with chunks of soda bread, toasted muffins or well-risen cheese scones, a good broth makes a great meal.

Warming toddies are the best body-warmers. The old favourite, whisky toddy, consists of a tot of whisky, several slices of lemon, a good squeeze of lemon juice and a couple of spoons of honey topped up with boiling water. Renowned for soothing a sore throat and clearing the head, the warm whisky has a soporific effect. For a modern, alcohol-free alternative, flavour a toddy with a few sprigs of fresh or dried rosemary and slices of orange and honey. Thin slices of fresh root ginger, lemon and honey make a punchy toddy, while hot apple juice, orange slices, cinnamon and honey make a warming cup that can be spiked with a little brandy for an extra kick.

Wonderful winter salads

An eclectic approach introduces the winter salad as a celebration of flavour, form and texture. Judicious use of pulses, whether soaked and cooked for the appropriate time, or pre-cooked in a can, gives a salad the protein boost it needs to make it more satisfying for winter appetites. Spices, seeds and preserved produce transform diced roots and tubers; nutty oils and rich vinegar dress without masking the flavour of the salad; and hot toppings transform salads into seriously good main courses.

PARING, DICING OR SHREDDING
Cutting techniques make all the difference to the finished dish. Potatoes, carrots and swedes can be cooked until tender, and diced when warm or cool for winter salads; opt for large or small dice depending on the texture required.

- Peel, finely dice and pan-fry potatoes, or par-boiled Jerusalem artichokes, in a little sunflower oil, stirring frequently, until browned and tender but firm. Season and toss with cold ingredients just before serving.

- Use a vegetable peeler to pare carrots into ribbons, then soak these in iced water until they curl. Toss them with a sweet-sour dressing flavoured with orange, and roasted fennel seeds just before serving.

- Finely slice or dice canned water chestnuts, or cut them into thin strips, and add them to tender cooked vegetables or winter greens for a super-crunchy texture.

ALTERNATIVE GREENS

When the light salad leaves of summer are out of season, it is time to turn to the greens that are in favour. Cabbages come in many varieties, and the paler ones are more suited to making variations on coleslaw.

- Finely shred wedges of firm winter cabbage, using the heart rather than the outer leaves; white and red cabbage are delicious shredded finely or coarsely.

- Use bean sprouts for bulk, texture and a light flavour with the more expensive leaves such as rocket (arugula), mizuna or watercress.

FRUIT FLAVOURS

Citrus scents are a boon to the winter salad maker, and exotic fruits are available from hotter climates. Use them in dressings to replace the vinegar, or sliced in the dish itself, to add an extra zing, and to complement the flavour of cold meats.

- Pomegranate seeds are delicious in all sorts of salads. Try them with pan-fried poultry, bacon, pancetta or pork strips; tangy goat's cheese or lively blue cheese; crunchy red cabbage and finely cut raw onion; or chickpeas, barley or wheat.

- Finely slice and then dice thin-skinned winter lemons and limes to bring brilliant bursts of flavour to all sorts of salads. Remove pips (seeds) when slicing the fruit. This is especially good with smoked fish, chickpeas or pan-fried diced gammon.

- Chopped dried apricots and dates are excellent with cheese, poultry or salami and other preserved meats. Other kinds of preserved fruits available include mangoes, apple slices, banana chips and papayas.

HOT DRESSING TIPS

Try tossing a full-flavoured hot dressing into cold ingredients when serving a salad.

- Fry diced bacon until crisp in a little sunflower oil. Remove from the pan with a slotted spoon and cook chopped garlic, a little chopped onion and shredded orange rind in the fat remaining in the pan for a few seconds. Whisk in some balsamic vinegar, freshly ground black pepper, a good pinch of sugar and a little mustard. Whisk in a little olive oil and bring to the boil. Remove from the heat, then drizzle over finely shredded Brussels sprouts or green cabbage and bean sprouts. Sprinkle with the bacon.

- Make a hot chilli dressing by cooking a finely chopped seeded fresh green chilli in a little olive oil with chopped garlic and grated lime rind. Whisk in lime juice, olive oil, seasoning and a little sugar or honey. Remove from the heat when hot. Good with poultry, fish, cheese or root vegetables.

TEMPTING TOPPINGS

The ubiquitous croutons are good on salads, but there are alternatives that turn the simplest vegetable combinations into substantial snacks or meals.

- Cut Welsh rarebit (cheese on toast) into neat squares and serve on a salad of white cabbage, carrot and watercress.

- Grill goat's cheese on slices of French baton or on English muffins. Cut the muffins into little wedges and serve with a salad of coarsely grated carrot and mixed sprouted seeds.

- Grill mashed canned sardines with garlic on thin toast and cut into fingers as a topping for potato salad. Cut the potatoes into fingers, rather than dice, and toss with an olive oil and lemon dressing, adding plenty of grated lemon rind to the dressing.

- Serve small bite-sized meatballs as a salad topping – good with greens or roots.

The thing about puddings

Call them old-fashioned but, in truth, hot puddings have never gone out of favour. We swoon at the first burst of aromatic steam from one of those peculiarly British savoury puddings, filled with steak and kidney, chicken scented with sage and lemon, or bacon and onion. We crave sweet puddings – light golden sponge trickling with treacle or mysteriously dark with chocolate; or fluffy suet pastry speckled with succulent dried fruits or swirled with fruity jam, topped with steaming vanilla custard.

PUDDING PERFECTION

Sponge puddings are amazingly simple to make. The ingredients can be beaten in stages, or at one go, using an electric beater, then spooned into a large cooking basin, covered with foil and steamed for 1–1½ hours.

Suet (chilled, grated shortening) pastry requires no rubbing, layering or folding, just mixing and rolling out. It can be filled and rolled up Swiss-roll style, or used to line a basin and filled. Everyone thinks of steaming as the main method of cooking for suet puddings, but they cook wonderfully well in the oven, becoming spongy and forming a light but crisp golden crust when baked. Fillings for baked puddings should be pre-cooked or quick to cook, as the baking time is far shorter than steaming (about 45 minutes). The pastry can be covered the whole time it is in the oven, but uncovering it for the final 15 minutes or so allows it to brown.

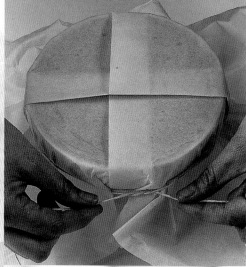

SO-SIMPLE SUET PASTRY

- Always use self-raising (self-rising) flour, or baking powder with plain (all-purpose) flour. Unlike other pastries, suet pastry relies on the raising agent for its light texture.

- Stir the suet into the flour, then mix in just enough water or milk to make a soft but not sticky dough.

- Roll the dough out lightly on a well-floured surface – the cooler it stays and the less it is handled, the lighter it will be.

- When lining a basin or bowl, save about a third for the lid, then roll out the rest of the pastry about 10cm | 4in larger than the top of the basin. Dust the pastry lightly with flour and fold into quarters, then place this wedge of pastry in the basin, with the point in the middle of the base. Open out the pastry to line the basin, leaving the excess pastry overhanging the edge. When the pudding is filled, roll out the reserved pastry into a round large enough to cover the filling, and place it on top, pressing it lightly to the rim. Brush the edge with water and fold the overhanging pastry over the edge to seal in the filling.

- For a roly-poly, roll out the pastry to about 5mm | ¼in thick and spread with filling, leaving a border of about 2.5cm | 1in around the edge. Fold the edge over the filling and brush with a little water before rolling up the pastry and filling.

- Wrap a roly-poly in greased baking parchment and foil for cooking, keeping it loose to allow the pastry to rise, but folding the foil firmly together to keep the moisture in.

Tangy
and Appetizing

As the days get shorter and colder, appetites sharpen.
Enjoy first courses and side dishes that make the most of
the new season's root vegetables and lift salads with the
energizing flavours of citrus and ground spices.

Root vegetables form the base of this chunky and filling minestrone-style soup. Vary the vegetables according to what you have to hand.

WINTER FARMHOUSE SOUP

INGREDIENTS
serves four

30ml | 2 tbsp olive oil

1 onion, roughly chopped

3 carrots, cut into large chunks

175–200g | 6–7oz turnips, cut into chunks

175g | 6oz swede (rutabaga) cut into chunks

400g | 14oz can chopped Italian tomatoes

15ml | 1 tbsp tomato purée (paste)

5ml | 1 tsp dried mixed herbs

5ml | 1 tsp dried oregano

50g | 2oz dried (bell) peppers, washed and thinly sliced (optional)

1.5 litres | 2¹/₂ pints | 6¹/₄ cups vegetable stock or water

50g | 2oz | ¹/₂ cup dried macaroni

400g | 14 oz can red kidney beans, rinsed and drained

30ml | 2 tbsp chopped fresh flat leaf parsley

sea salt and ground black pepper

freshly grated Parmesan cheese to serve

1 Heat the olive oil in a large pan, add the onion and cook over a low heat for about 5 minutes, until softened. Add the carrot, turnip, swede chunks, canned chopped tomatoes, tomato purée, dried mixed herbs, dried oregano and dried peppers, if using. Stir in a little salt and plenty of pepper to taste.

2 Pour in the vegetable stock or water and bring to the boil. Stir well, cover the pan, then lower the heat and simmer for 30 minutes, stirring occasionally.

3 Add the pasta to the pan and bring quickly to the boil, stirring. Lower the heat and simmer, uncovered, for about 8 minutes, until the pasta is only just tender, or according to the instructions on the packet. Stir frequently.

4 Stir in the kidney beans. Heat through for 2–3 minutes, then remove the pan from the heat and stir in the parsley. Taste the soup for seasoning. Serve hot in warmed soup bowls, with grated cheese handed around separately.

Vegetables roasted in olive oil give this winter soup a wonderful depth of flavour. You can use other vegetables if you wish, or adapt the quantities, depending on what you have to hand.

ROASTED ROOT VEGETABLE SOUP

1 Preheat the oven to 200°C|400°F|Gas 6. Put the olive oil into a large bowl. Add the prepared vegetables and toss until coated in the oil.

2 Spread out the vegetables in a single layer on one large or two small baking sheets. Tuck the bay leaves and the thyme and rosemary sprigs among the vegetables.

3 Roast the vegetables for about 50 minutes, until tender, turning them occasionally to make sure they brown evenly. Remove from the oven, discard the herbs and transfer the vegetables to a large pan.

4 Pour the stock into the pan and bring to the boil. Reduce the heat, season to taste, then simmer for 10 minutes. Transfer the soup to a food processor or blender (or use a hand blender) and process for a few minutes, until thick and smooth.

5 Return the soup to the pan to heat through. Season and serve with a swirl of sour cream. Garnish each serving with a sprig of thyme.

COOK'S TIP Dried herbs can be used in place of fresh; sprinkle 2.5ml|1/2 tsp of each over the vegetables in step 2.

INGREDIENTS
serves six

50ml | 2fl oz | 1/4 cups olive oil

1 small butternut squash, peeled, seeded and cubed

2 carrots, cut into thick rounds

1 large parsnip, cubed

1 small swede (rutabaga), cubed

2 leeks, thickly sliced

1 onion, quartered

3 bay leaves

4 thyme sprigs, plus extra to garnish

3 rosemary sprigs

1.2 litres | 2 pints | 5 cups vegetable stock

salt and ground black pepper

sour cream, to serve

These versatile and delicious filo pastry parcels are an excellent way of using up small pieces of cooked turkey – a useful idea if you have lots of turkey leftovers.

TURKEY and CRANBERRY PURSES

INGREDIENTS
serves six

450g | 1lb cooked turkey, cut into chunks

115g | 4oz | 1 cup diced Brie cheese

30ml | 2 tbsp cranberry sauce

30ml | 2 tbsp chopped fresh parsley

9 sheets of filo pastry, each measuring 45 x 28cm | 18 x 11in, thawed if frozen

50g | 2oz | 1¼ cups butter, melted

salt and ground black pepper

1 Preheat the oven to 200°C | 400°F | Gas 6. Place the turkey, Brie, cranberry sauce and chopped parsley in a small mixing bowl and mix well. Season with salt and pepper.

2 Cut the sheets of filo in half widthways and trim to make 18 squares. Keeping the remaining filo covered with clear film (plastic wrap) to prevent it from drying out, layer three pieces of pastry together, brushing each layer with a little melted butter. Repeat with the remaining filo squares to make 6 stacks.

3 Divide the turkey mixture evenly among the pastry stacks, making a neat pile in the centre of each piece. Gather up the pastry to enclose the filling in neat bundles. Place on a baking sheet, brush with melted butter and bake for about 20 minutes, or until the pastry is crisp and golden.

COOK'S TIP These little parcels can be made with a variety of fillings:
HAM AND CHEDDAR PURSES Replace the turkey with ham and use Cheddar cheese in place of the Brie. A fruit chutney would make a good alternative to the cranberry sauce.
CHICKEN AND STILTON PURSES Use cooked, diced chicken breast portions, white Stilton cheese and mango chutney.
GOAT'S CHEESE AND CELERY PURSES Use chopped celery and almonds, sautéed in a little butter, goat's cheese and chopped fresh figs.

Some of the most delicious dishes are also the simplest to make. Serve this popular pâté with warmed Melba toast as a first course, or for a light lunch with wholemeal toast.

SMOKED MACKEREL PÂTÉ

1 Break up the mackerel and put it in a food processor. Add the cream cheese, garlic, lemon juice and herbs.

2 Process the mixture until it is fairly smooth but still has a slightly chunky texture, then add Worcestershire sauce, salt and cayenne pepper to taste. Whizz to mix, then spoon the pâté into a dish, cover with clear film (plastic wrap) and chill. Garnish with chives and serve with Melba toast.

COOK'S TIP To make Melba toast, place some ready-sliced bread under a preheated grill (broiler) until browned on both sides. Cut off the crusts, and carefully slide the knife between the toasted edges to split the bread. Grill the uncooked sides again until the edges curl. The toast can be made in advance, and then reheated in a low oven.

VARIATION Use peppered mackerel fillets for a more piquant flavour. This pâté can also be made with smoked haddock or kipper fillets.

INGREDIENTS
serves six

4 smoked mackerel fillets, skinned

225g | 8oz | 1 cup cream cheese

1–2 garlic cloves, finely chopped

juice of 1 lemon

30ml | 2 tbsp chopped fresh chervil, parsley or chives

15ml | 1 tbsp Worcestershire sauce

salt and cayenne pepper

fresh chives, to garnish

warmed Melba toast, to serve

The combination of sweet beetroot, zesty orange and warm cinnamon in this salad is surprisingly delicious, and provides a lovely burst of colour in a winter buffet spread. It can be made with freshly steamed or pre-cooked beetroot.

BEETROOT SALAD with ORANGES

INGREDIENTS
serves four to six

675g | 1¹/₂lb beetroot (beet), steamed or boiled, then peeled

1 orange, peeled and sliced

30ml | 2 tbsp orange flower water

15ml | 1 tbsp sugar

5ml | 1 tsp ground cinnamon

salt and ground black pepper

1 Quarter the cooked beetroot, then slice the quarters. Arrange the beetroot on a plate with the orange slices or toss them together in a bowl.

2 Gently heat the orange flower water with the sugar, stir in the cinnamon and season to taste.

3 Pour the sweet mixture over the beetroot and orange salad and chill for at least 1 hour before serving.

COOK'S TIP To cook raw beetroot, always leave the skin on, and trim off only the tops of the leaf stalks. Cook in boiling water or steam over rapidly boiling water for 1–2 hours, depending on size. Small beetroots are tender in about 1 hour, medium roots take 1–1¹/₂ hours, and larger roots can take up to 2 hours.

Cook this vibrantly coloured dish in the oven at the same time as a pork casserole or a roast joint of meat for a simple, easy-to-prepare meal.

BRAISED RED CABBAGE with BEETROOT

INGREDIENTS
serves six to eight

675g | 1½lb red cabbage

1 Spanish (Bermuda) onion, thinly sliced

30ml | 2 tbsp olive oil

2 tart eating apples, peeled, cored and sliced

300ml | ½ pint | 1¼ cups vegetable stock

60ml | 4 tbsp red wine vinegar

375g | 13oz raw beetroot (beet), peeled and coarsely grated

sea salt and ground black pepper

1 Cut the red cabbage into fine shreds, discarding any tough outer leaves and the core, and place in an ovenproof dish.

2 Place the thinly sliced onion and the olive oil in a frying pan and sauté until the onion is soft and golden.

3 Preheat the oven to 190°C | 375°F | Gas 5. Stir the apple slices, vegetable stock and wine vinegar into the onion, then transfer to the dish. Season with salt and pepper and cover.

4 Cook the cabbage for 1 hour. Stir in the beetroot, recover the dish and cook for a further 20–30 minutes, or until the cabbage and beetroot are tender.

COOK'S TIP When buying any type of cabbage, choose one that is firm and heavy for its size. The leaves should look healthy. Avoid any with curling leaves or blemishes.

This traditional Irish dish is the ultimate comfort food. Made with potatoes, onions and buttermilk, it is enriched with a wickedly indulgent amount of butter.

CHAMP

1 Boil the potatoes in lightly salted water for 20–25 minutes, until tender. Drain and mash with a fork until smooth.

2 Place the milk, spring onions and half the butter in a small pan and set over a low heat until just simmering. Cook for 2–3 minutes, until the butter has melted and the spring onions have softened.

3 Beat the milk mixture into the mashed potato using a wooden spoon. Beat in the buttermilk or crème fraîche until the mixture is light and fluffy. Reheat gently, adding salt and pepper to taste.

4 Turn the potato into a warmed serving dish and make a well in the centre with a spoon. Place the remaining butter in the well and let it melt. Serve immediately, sprinkled with extra spring onion.

VARIATIONS

COLCANNON This is another Irish speciality. Follow the main recipe, using half the butter. Cook about 500g | 1¼lb finely shredded green cabbage or kale in a little water until just tender, drain thoroughly and then beat into the creamed potato. This is delicious with sausages and grilled ham or bacon. It may also be fried in butter and then browned lightly under the grill (broiler).

CLAPSHOT To make this Scottish dish, halve the quantity of potato and replace with an equal weight (or slightly more) of swede (rutabaga). Use less butter and omit the buttermilk. Season with black pepper and plenty of freshly grated nutmeg. Traditionally, a chopped onion would be cooked with the potatoes and swede.

INGREDIENTS
serves four to six

1kg | 2¼lb boiling potatoes, cut into chunks

250ml | 8fl oz | 1 cup milk

1 bunch spring onions (scallions), thinly sliced, plus extra to garnish

115g | 4oz | ½ cup slightly salted butter

60ml | 4 tbsp buttermilk or crème fraîche

salt and ground black pepper

Nourishing and Vibrant

Filling fare such as beans and potatoes are combined
with the zing of chilli, ginger and warming spices to
make easy winter meals that will satisfy both
the stomach and the tastebuds.

This is an easy dish, as black-eyed beans do not need to be soaked overnight. With spring onions and loads of aromatic dill, it is refreshing and healthy.

WARM SALAD with BLACK-EYED BEANS

INGREDIENTS
serves four

275g | 10oz | 1½ cups black-eyed beans (peas)

5 spring onions (scallions), sliced

a large handful of rocket (arugula) leaves, chopped if large

small cos (romaine) lettuce leaves

45–60ml | 3–4 tbsp chopped fresh dill

150ml | ¼ pint | ⅔ cup extra virgin olive oil

juice of 1 lemon, or more

10–12 black olives

salt and ground black pepper

1 Rinse and drain the beans, tip them into a pan and pour in cold water to cover. Bring to the boil, and strain immediately. Put them back in the pan with fresh cold water to cover, and add a pinch of salt. This will make their skins harder and prevent them from disintegrating when they are cooked.

2 Bring the beans to the boil, then lower the heat slightly and cook them until they are soft but not mushy. They will take 20–30 minutes, so keep an eye on them.

3 Drain the beans, reserving 75–90ml | 5–6 tbsp of the cooking liquid. Tip the beans into a large salad bowl, then add the remaining ingredients, including the reserved liquid, and mix well. Serve straight away as a warm salad, and serve with plenty of fresh, crusty bread.

VARIATION Rocket leaves have a peppery taste that complements the flavour of the beans, but watercress, with its equally strong flavour, may be used as an alternative.

Sweet parsnips, nutty chickpeas, zingy chilli and ginger paste combine to make a really tasty and filling dish, and will make a main meal when served with warm naan bread or chapatis.

ZINGY PARSNIP and CHICKPEA CURRY

1 Put the soaked chickpeas in a pan, cover with cold water and bring to the boil. Boil vigorously for 10 minutes, then reduce the heat so that the water boils steadily. Cook for 1–1½ hours, or until the chickpeas are tender. (The cooking time will depend on how long the chickpeas have been stored.) Drain and set aside.

2 Set 10ml | 2 tsp of the finely chopped garlic aside, then place the remainder in a food processor or blender with the onion, ginger and half the chopped chillies. Add 75ml | 5 tbsp water and process to make a smooth paste.

3 Heat the oil in a frying pan and cook the cumin seeds for 30 seconds. Stir in the coriander seeds, turmeric, chilli powder or paprika and the ground cashew nuts. Mix in the ginger paste and cook, stirring frequently, until the water begins to evaporate. Add the tomatoes and stir-fry for 2–3 minutes.

4 Mix in the cooked chickpeas and parsnip chunks with 450ml | ¾ pint | scant 2 cups water, a little salt and plenty of black pepper. Bring to the boil, stir, then simmer, uncovered, for 15–20 minutes, until the parsnips are completely tender.

5 Reduce the liquid, if necessary, by bringing the sauce to the boil and then boiling fiercely until the sauce is thick. Add the ground roasted cumin with more salt and lime juice to taste. Stir in the reserved garlic and green chilli, and cook for a further 1–2 minutes. Scatter the fresh coriander leaves and toasted cashew nuts over and serve straight away with yogurt and warmed naan bread or chapatis.

INGREDIENTS
serves four

200g | 7oz | 1 cup dried chickpeas, soaked overnight in cold water, then drained

7 garlic cloves, finely chopped

1 small onion, chopped

5cm | 2in piece fresh root ginger, chopped

2 green chillies, seeded and chopped

60ml | 4 tbsp sunflower oil

5ml | 1 tsp cumin seeds

10ml | 2 tsp ground coriander seeds

5ml | 1 tsp ground turmeric

2.5–5ml | ½–1 tsp chilli powder or mild paprika

50g | 2oz | ½ cup cashew nuts, toasted and ground

250g | 9oz tomatoes, peeled and chopped

900g | 2lb parsnips, cut into chunks

5ml | 1 tsp ground roasted cumin seeds

juice of 1 lime, to taste

chopped fresh coriander (cilantro) leaves and toasted whole cashew nuts, to garnish

These golden-brown, crisp potato cakes flavoured with onion, bacon and herbs are irresistible.

BACON and HERB RÖSTI

INGREDIENTS
serves four

450g | 1lb potatoes, left whole and unpeeled

30ml | 2 tbsp olive oil

1 red onion, finely chopped

4 back (lean) bacon rashers (strips), rinded and diced

15ml | 1 tbsp potato flour

30ml | 2 tbsp chopped fresh mixed herbs

salt and ground black pepper

fresh parsley sprigs, to garnish

1 Lightly grease a baking sheet. Par-boil the potatoes in a pan of lightly salted, boiling water for about 6 minutes. Drain the potatoes and set aside to cool slightly.

2 Once cool enough to handle, peel the potatoes and coarsely grate them into a bowl. Set aside.

3 Heat 15ml | 1 tbsp of the oil in a frying pan, add the onion and bacon, and cook gently for 5 minutes, stirring occasionally. Preheat the oven to 220°C | 425°F | Gas 7.

4 Remove the pan from the heat. Stir the onion mixture, remaining oil, potato flour, herbs and seasoning into the grated potatoes and mix well.

5 Divide the mixture into 8 small piles and spoon them on to the prepared baking sheet, leaving a little space between each one.

6 Bake for 20–25 minutes until the rösti are crisp and golden brown. Serve immediately, garnished with sprigs of fresh parsley.

Subtly spiced with curry powder, turmeric, coriander and mild chilli powder, this rich gratin is substantial enough to serve on its own for lunch or supper. It also makes a good accompaniment to a larger meal.

VEGETABLE GRATIN with INDIAN SPICES

1 Thinly slice the potatoes, sweet potatoes and celeriac, using a sharp knife or the slicing attachment on a food processor. Immediately place the vegetables in a bowl of cold water to prevent them from discolouring.

2 Preheat the oven to 180°C | 350°F | Gas 4. Heat half the butter in a heavy pan, add the curry powder, turmeric and coriander and half of the chilli powder. Cook for 2 minutes, then leave to cool slightly. Drain the vegetables, then pat dry with kitchen paper. Place in a bowl, add the spice mixture and the shallots, and mix well.

3 Arrange the vegetables in a gratin dish, seasoning between the layers. Mix together the cream and milk, pour the mixture over the vegetables, then sprinkle the remaining chilli powder on top.

4 Cover with greaseproof (waxed) paper and bake for about 45 minutes. Remove the greaseproof paper, dot with the remaining butter and bake for a further 50 minutes, until the top is golden. Serve garnished with chopped fresh parsley.

COOK'S TIP The cream adds richness to this gratin. Use semi-skimmed (low-fat) milk if you prefer.

INGREDIENTS
serves four

2 large potatoes, total weight about 450g | 1lb

2 sweet potatoes, total weight about 275g | 10oz

175g | 6oz celeriac

15ml | 1 tbsp unsalted (sweet) butter

5ml | 1 tsp curry powder

5ml | 1 tsp ground turmeric

2.5ml | 1/2 tsp ground coriander

5ml | 1 tsp mild chilli powder

3 shallots, chopped

150ml | 1/4 pint | 2/3 cup single (light) cream

150ml | 1/4 pint | 2/3 cup milk

salt and ground black pepper

chopped fresh flat leaf parsley, to garnish

Serve this hearty butter-bean dish with grills, roasts, or fish. It is substantial enough to be served on its own, with a leafy salad and fresh, crusty bread. Bean dishes like this one often include a spicy sausage, such as Spanish chorizo. This can be added with the onion to lend its flavour to the whole dish.

TAGINE of BUTTER BEANS with OLIVES

INGREDIENTS
serves four

115g | 4oz | 2/3 cup butter (lima) beans, soaked overnight

30–45ml | 2–3 tbsp olive oil

1 onion, chopped

2–3 garlic cloves, crushed

25g | 1oz fresh root ginger, peeled and chopped

pinch of saffron threads

16 cherry tomatoes

generous pinch of sugar

handful of fleshy black olives, pitted

5ml | 1 tsp ground cinnamon

5ml | 1 tsp paprika

small bunch of flat leaf parsley

salt and ground black pepper

1 Rinse the beans and place them in a large pan with plenty of water. Bring to the boil and boil for about 10 minutes, then reduce the heat and simmer gently for 1–1½ hours, until tender. Drain the beans and refresh under cold water.

2 Heat the olive oil in a heavy pan. Add the onion, garlic and ginger and cook for about 10 minutes, or until softened but not browned. Stir in the saffron threads, followed by the cherry tomatoes and a sprinkling of sugar.

3 As the tomatoes begin to soften, stir in the butter beans. When the tomatoes have heated through, stir in the olives, ground cinnamon and paprika. Season to taste and sprinkle over the parsley. Serve immediately.

COOK'S TIP
If you are in a hurry, you could use two 400g | 14oz cans of butter beans for this tagine. Make sure you rinse the beans well, as canned beans tend to be salty.

Hearty and Satisfying

Winter is the season for indulging the appetite in truly fulfilling dishes while entertaining friends and family. Rich gravies and tangy sauces accompany succulent roast meats and fish, pies and casseroles.

This aromatic dish originated in India. For a colourful garnish, add some finely sliced red onion or a little red onion marmalade.

KEDGEREE with SMOKED HADDOCK

INGREDIENTS
serves four

450g | 1lb undyed smoked haddock fillet

750ml | 1¼ pints | 3 cups milk

2 bay leaves

½ lemon, sliced

50g | 2oz | ¼ cup butter

1 onion, chopped

2.5ml | ½ tsp ground turmeric

5ml | 1 tsp mild Madras curry powder

2 green cardamom pods

350g | 12oz | 1¾ cups basmati or long grain rice, washed and drained

4 hard-boiled eggs (not too hard), roughly chopped

150ml | ¼ pint | ⅔ cup single (light) cream or Greek (US strained plain) yogurt (optional)

30ml | 2 tbsp chopped fresh parsley

salt and ground black pepper

1 Put the haddock in a shallow pan and add the milk, bay leaves and lemon slices. Poach gently for 8–10 minutes, until the haddock flakes easily when tested with the tip of a sharp knife. Strain the milk into a jug (pitcher), discarding the bay leaves and lemon slices. Remove the skin from the flesh of the haddock and flake the flesh into large pieces. Keep hot until required.

2 Melt the butter in the pan, add the onion and cook over a low heat for about 3 minutes, until softened. Stir in the turmeric, curry powder and cardamom pods and fry for 1 minute.

3 Add the rice, stirring to coat it well with the butter. Pour in the reserved milk, stir and bring to the boil. Lower the heat and simmer the rice for 10–12 minutes, until all the milk has been absorbed and the rice is tender. Season to taste, going easy on the salt.

4 Gently stir in the fish and hard-boiled eggs, with the cream or yogurt, if using. Sprinkle with the parsley and serve.

VARIATION Use smoked and poached fresh salmon for a delicious change.

This is a classic dish. It has layers of flavour, and the herbs add enticing aromas. Although it is made with economical ingredients (mussels are cheap compared to fish), it always produces spectacular results and is well worth the time it takes to prepare the seafood.

MUSSEL and RICE PILAFF

1 Discard any mussels that are not tightly shut, or which fail to snap shut when tapped. Place the remainder in a large heavy pan. Add about 1/3 of the onion slices, then pour in half of the wine and 150ml | 1/4 pint | 2/3 cup of the hot water. Cover and cook over a high heat for about 5 minutes, shaking the pan occasionally, until the mussels start to open.

2 Transfer the open mussels to a colander and collect their liquid in a bowl. Discard any mussels that remain closed. Shell most of the mussels, but keep a dozen or so large ones in their shells for decorative purposes. Let the liquid remaining in the pan settle, then carefully strain it through a lined sieve. Do the same with the liquid from the bowl, which drained from the cooked mussels.

3 Heat the olive oil in a heavy pan, add the remaining onion slices and spring onions, and sauté over a medium heat until both start to turn golden. Add the garlic and oregano.

4 As soon as the garlic becomes aromatic, add the rice and stir briefly to coat the grains in the oil. Add the remaining wine, stirring until it has been absorbed, then stir in the remaining 300ml | 1/2 pint | 1 1/4 cups water, the reserved mussel liquid and the chopped parsley. Season with salt and pepper, then cover and cook gently for about 5 minutes, stirring occasionally.

5 Add the mussels, including the ones in their shells. Sprinkle in half of the dill and mix well. If necessary, add a little more hot water. Cover and cook gently for 5–6 minutes more, until the rice is cooked but still has a bit of bite at the centre of the grain. Sprinkle the remaining dill on top and serve with a green salad.

INGREDIENTS
serves four

1.6kg | 3 1/2lb mussels, scrubbed and bearded

2 onions, thinly sliced

2 glasses white wine, about 350ml | 12fl oz | 1 1/2 cups

450ml | 3/4 pint | scant 2 cups hot water

150ml | 1/4 pint | 2/3 cup extra virgin olive oil

5–6 spring onions (scallions), chopped

2 garlic cloves, chopped

large pinch of dried oregano

200g | 7oz | 1 cup long grain rice

45ml | 3 tbsp finely chopped fresh flat leaf parsley

45–60ml | 3–4 tbsp chopped fresh dill

salt and ground black pepper

The aroma of orange pervades many classic dishes, and the juice adds a distinctive flavour to wonderful fish recipes like this one. Red mullet is one of the fish that is still available from the Mediterranean in winter.

BAKED RED MULLET with ORANGES

INGREDIENTS
serves four

a few sprigs of fresh dill

4 large red mullet, total weight 1–1.2kg | 2¹/₄–2¹/₂lb, cleaned

2 large oranges, halved

¹/₂ lemon

60ml | 4 tbsp extra virgin olive oil

30ml | 2 tbsp pine nuts

salt

1 Place some fresh dill in the cavity of each fish, and lay the fish in a baking dish, preferably one that can be taken straight to the table.

2 Set half an orange aside and squeeze the rest, along with the lemon. Mix the juice with the olive oil, then pour the mixture over the fish. Turn the fish so that they are evenly coated in the marinade, then cover and leave in a cool place to marinate for 1–2 hours, spooning the marinade over the fish occasionally.

3 Preheat the oven to 180°C | 350°F | Gas 4. Sprinkle a little salt over each fish. Slice the reserved orange half into thin rounds, then cut each round into quarters. Place two or three of these orange wedges over each fish. Bake for 20 minutes, then remove the dish from the oven, baste the fish with the juices and sprinkle the pine nuts over. Return the dish to the oven and bake for 10–15 minutes more.

VARIATION Bake oily sea fish such as herring and mackerel in a marinade made with lemons for a refreshing change.

A filling casserole of wonderfully tender chicken, root vegetables and lentils, finished with crème fraîche, mustard and tarragon, will warm you up on a cold winter's day.

CHICKEN CASSEROLE with WINTER VEGETABLES

INGREDIENTS
serves four

350g | 12oz onions

350g | 12oz leeks

225g | 8oz carrots

450g | 1lb swede (rutabaga)

30ml | 2 tbsp olive oil

4 chicken portions, about 900g | 2lb total weight

115g | 4oz | 1/2 cup green lentils

475ml | 16fl oz | 2 cups chicken stock

300ml | 1/2 pint | 1¼ cups apple juice

10ml | 2 tsp cornflour (cornstarch)

45ml | 3 tbsp crème fraîche

10ml | 2 tsp wholegrain mustard

30ml | 2 tbsp chopped fresh tarragon

salt and ground black pepper

fresh tarragon sprigs, to garnish

1 Preheat the oven to 190°C | 375°F | Gas 5. Prepare and chop the vegetables.

2 Heat the oil in a large flameproof casserole. Season the chicken portions and brown them in the hot oil until golden. Remove the chicken from the pan.

3 Add the onions to the casserole and cook for 5 minutes, stirring, until they begin to soften and colour. Add the leeks, carrots, swede and lentils to the casserole and stir over a medium heat for 2 minutes.

4 Return the chicken to the pan, then add the stock, apple juice and seasoning. Bring to the boil and cover tightly. Cook in the oven for 50–60 minutes, or until the chicken and lentils are tender.

5 Place the casserole on the hob (stovetop) over a medium heat. In a small bowl, blend the cornflour with about 30ml | 2 tbsp water to make a smooth paste, and add to the casserole with the crème fraîche, wholegrain mustard and chopped tarragon. Adjust the seasoning, then simmer gently for about 2 minutes, stirring, until thickened slightly. Serve, garnished with tarragon sprigs.

COOK'S TIP Chop the vegetables into similarly sized pieces so that they cook evenly. Organic vegetables do not need peeling.

A succulent roast goose is the classic centrepiece for a traditional winter family dinner. Juicy red cabbage cooked with leeks, and braised fennel are tasty and colourful accompaniments.

MARMALADE-GLAZED GOOSE with STUFFING

1 Preheat the oven to 200°C | 400°F | Gas 6. Prick the skin of the goose all over and season it inside and out. Mix the apple, onion and sage leaves together and spoon the mixture into the parson's nose end of the goose.

2 To make the stuffing, melt the butter or oil in a large pan and cook the onion for about 5 minutes, or until softened but not coloured. Remove the pan from the heat and stir in the marmalade, chopped prunes, Madeira, breadcrumbs and chopped sage.

3 Stuff the neck end of the goose with the stuffing. Sew up the bird or secure it with skewers to prevent the stuffing from escaping during cooking.

4 Place the goose in a large roasting pan. Butter a piece of foil and use to cover the goose loosely, then roast in the preheated oven for 2 hours.

5 Baste the goose frequently during cooking and remove any excess fat from the pan as necessary, using a small ladle or serving spoon. (Strain, cool and chill the fat in a covered container: it is excellent for roasting potatoes.)

6 Remove the foil from the goose and brush the melted ginger marmalade over the goose, then roast for 30–40 minutes more, or until cooked through. To check the goose is cooked, pierce the thick part of the thigh with a metal skewer; the juices will run clear when the bird is cooked. Remove from the oven and cover with foil, then leave to stand for 15 minutes before carving.

INGREDIENTS
serves eight

4.5kg | 10lb goose

1 cooking apple, peeled, cored and cut into eighths

1 large onion, cut into eighths

bunch of fresh sage, plus extra to garnish

30ml/2 tbsp ginger marmalade, melted

salt and ground black pepper

for the stuffing

25g | 1oz | 2 tbsp butter or 30ml | 2 tbsp olive oil

1 onion, finely chopped

15ml | 1 tbsp ginger marmalade

450g | 1lb | 2 cups ready-to-eat prunes, chopped

45ml | 3 tbsp Madeira

225g | 8oz | 4 cups fresh white or wholemeal (whole-wheat) breadcrumbs

30ml | 2 tbsp chopped fresh sage

William the Conqueror introduced cider-making to England from Normandy in 1066. This wonderful old West Country ham glazed with cider is traditionally served with cranberry sauce.

SOMERSET CIDER-GLAZED HAM

1 Weigh the ham and calculate the cooking time at 20 minutes per 450g | 1lb, and then place it in a large pan. Stud the onion or onions with half of the cloves and add to the pan with the bay leaves and peppercorns.

2 Add 1.2 litres | 2 pints | 5 cups of the cider and enough water to cover the ham. Heat until simmering and then carefully skim off the scum that rises to the surface, using a large spoon or ladle. Time the cooking from the moment the stock begins to simmer. Cover with a lid or foil and simmer gently for the calculated time. Towards the end of the cooking time, preheat the oven to 220°C | 425° | Gas 7.

3 Heat the sugar and remaining cider in a pan; stir until the sugar has dissolved. Simmer for 5 minutes to make a dark, sticky glaze. Remove the pan from the heat and leave to cool for 5 minutes. Lift the ham out of the pan, using a draining spoon and a large fork. Carefully and evenly, cut the rind from the ham, then score the fat into a neat diamond pattern. Place the ham in a roasting pan or ovenproof dish. Press a clove into the centre of each diamond, then carefully spoon over the glaze. Bake for 20–25 minutes, or until the fat is brown, glistening and crisp.

4 Simmer all the cranberry sauce ingredients in a heavy-based pan for 15–20 minutes, stirring frequently. Transfer the sauce to a jug. Serve the ham hot or cold, garnished with parsley and with the cranberry sauce.

VARIATION Use honey in place of the soft brown sugar for the glaze, and serve the ham with redcurrant sauce or jelly.

INGREDIENTS
serves eight to ten

2kg | 4^1/$_2$lb middle gammon joint

1 large or 2 small onions

about 30 whole cloves

3 bay leaves

10 black peppercorns

1.3 litres | 2^1/$_4$ pints | 5^2/$_3$ cups medium-dry cider

45ml | 3 tbsp soft light brown sugar

bunch of flat leaf parsley, to garnish

for the cranberry sauce

350g | 12oz | 3 cups cranberries

175g | 6oz | ^{3}/$_4$ cup soft light brown sugar

grated rind and juice of 2 clementines

30ml | 2 tbsp port

This hearty winter dish has a rich Guinness gravy and a herb pastry top. The Stilton adds a delicious creaminess but can be left out to make a less rich version of the pie.

CHESTNUT, STILTON and GUINNESS PIE

INGREDIENTS
serves four

115g | 4oz | 1 cup wholemeal (whole-wheat) flour

50g | 2oz | 4 tbsp unsalted (sweet) butter

30ml | 2 tbsp fresh thyme

30ml | 2 tbsp sunflower oil

2 large onions, chopped

500g | 1¼lb | 8 cups button (white) mushrooms

3 carrots and 1 parsnip, sliced

2 bay leaves

250ml | 8fl oz | 1 cup Guinness

120ml | 4fl oz | ½ cup vegetable stock

5ml | 1 tsp Worcestershire sauce

5ml | 1 tsp soft dark brown sugar

350g | 12oz | 3 cups canned chestnuts

30ml | 2 tbsp plain (all-purpose) flour

150g | 5oz | 1¼ cups Stilton cheese

salt and freshly ground black pepper

1 egg, beaten, or milk, to glaze

1 To make the pastry, rub together the flour, salt and butter until the mixture resembles fine breadcrumbs. Add half the thyme and enough water to form a soft dough. Turn out the dough on to a floured board or work surface and gently knead for 1 minute until a smooth dough forms. Wrap in clear film (plastic wrap) and chill for 30 minutes.

2 Meanwhile, to make the filling, heat the sunflower oil in a heavy pan and fry the onions for 5 minutes until softened, stirring occasionally. Halve the mushrooms, add and cook for a further 3 minutes or until just tender. Add the carrots, parsnip and the rest of the thyme, stir and cover the pan. Cook for three minutes until slightly softened.

3 Pour in the Guinness, vegetable stock and Worcestershire sauce, then add the sugar and seasoning. Simmer, covered, for 5 minutes, stirring occasionally. Halve the chestnuts and add.

4 Mix the flour to a paste with 30ml | 2 tbsp water. Add to the Guinness mixture and cook, uncovered, for 5 minutes, until the sauce thickens, stirring. Stir in the cheese and heat until melted, stirring constantly.

5 Preheat the oven to 220°C | 425° | Gas 7. Roll out the pastry to fit the top of a 1.5 litre | 2½ pint | 6¼ cup deep pie dish. Spoon the chestnut mixture into the dish. Dampen the edges of the dish and cover with the pastry. Seal, trim and crimp the edges. Cut a small slit in the top of the pie and use any surplus pastry to make pastry leaves. Brush with egg or milk and bake for 30 minutes until the pastry is golden.

Low in fat but high in flavour, venison is an excellent choice for a healthy, yet rich, casserole. Cranberries and orange bring fruitiness to this spicy recipe.

SPICY VENISON CASSEROLE

1 Heat the oil in a flameproof casserole. Add the onion and celery and sauté for about 5 minutes, until softened.

2 Meanwhile, mix the ground allspice with the flour and either spread the mixture out on a large plate or place in a large plastic bag. Toss a few pieces of venison at a time (to prevent them from becoming soggy) in the flour mixture until they are all lightly coated.

3 When the onion and celery are softened, remove from the casserole using a slotted spoon and set aside. Add the venison pieces to the casserole in batches and cook until browned and sealed on all sides.

4 Add the cranberries, orange rind and juice to the casserole along with the beef or venison stock and stir well. Return the vegetables and all the venison to the casserole and heat until simmering, then cover tightly and reduce the heat. Simmer for about 45 minutes, until the venison is tender, stirring occasionally.

5 Season to taste with salt and pepper before serving.

VARIATION Farmed venison is increasingly easy to find and is available at good butchers and many large supermarkets. It makes a rich and flavourful stew, but lean pork or braising steak could be used instead of the venison if you prefer. You could also replace the cranberries with pitted and halved prunes, and, for extra flavour, use either ale or stout instead of about half the stock.

INGREDIENTS
serves four

30ml | 2 tbsp olive oil

1 onion, chopped

2 celery stalks, sliced

10ml | 2 tsp ground allspice

15ml | 1 tbsp plain (all-purpose) flour

675g | 1 1/2lb stewing venison, cubed

225g | 8oz fresh or frozen cranberries

grated rind and juice of 1 orange

900ml | 1 1/2 pints | 3 3/4 cups beef or venison stock

salt and ground black pepper

Cassoulet is a very hearty, one-pot meal of white beans, fresh and preserved meats and sausage. Adding each meat at different stages to the simmering pot of beans and flavourings is crucial to the finished dish. This is a great dish to make in advance – traditionally it can go on bubbling for days.

BUTTER BEAN CASSOULET with DUCK

INGREDIENTS
serves six to eight

675g | 1¹/₂lb | 3³/₄ cups dried butter (lima) beans

2 large onions, sliced

6 large garlic cloves, crushed

3 bay leaves

10ml | 2 tsp dried thyme

2 whole cloves

60ml | 4 tbsp tomato purée (paste)

12 sun-dried tomatoes in oil, drained and roughly chopped

450g | 1lb smoked pancetta

60ml | 4 tbsp olive oil

4 boneless duck breasts

12 Toulouse or chunky Italian sausages

400g | 14oz can plum tomatoes

75g | 3oz | 1¹/₂ cups stale white breadcrumbs

salt and ground black pepper

1 Put the beans in a large bowl, cover with plenty of cold water and leave to soak for several hours or overnight.

2 Drain the beans well and tip into a large pan. Cover with fresh water and bring to the boil. Boil rapidly for 10 minutes to destroy any indigestible enzymes, then drain well and put into a large flameproof casserole. Add the onions, garlic, bay leaves, dried thyme, cloves, tomato purée and sun-dried tomatoes.

3 Trim the rind from the pancetta and cut into large pieces. Heat about 30ml | 2 tbsp of the oil in a frying pan and brown the pancetta in batches. Stir it into the casserole and add enough water to cover. Bring to the boil, then reduce the heat so that it just simmers. Cover and simmer for about 1¹/₂ hours, until the beans are tender.

4 Preheat the oven to 180°C | 350°F | Gas 4. Score the skin of the duck breasts, then cut each breast into large pieces. Cut each sausage into three pieces. Heat the remaining oil in a frying pan and fry the duck, skin side down, until golden-brown, then transfer to the casserole. Lightly fry the sausages in the remaining fat and stir into the beans with the canned tomatoes, adding salt and pepper to taste.

5 Sprinkle the breadcrumbs in an even layer over the surface of the cassoulet and bake for 45–60 minutes, or until a golden crust has formed. Serve warm.

Long, slow cooking is the trick to remember for good onion gravy, as this reduces and caramelizes the onions to create a wonderfully sweet flavour. Do not be alarmed by the number of onions – they reduce dramatically in volume during cooking.

SAUSAGES with MASH and ONION GRAVY

1 Heat the oil and butter in a large pan until foaming. Add the onions and mix well to coat them in the fat. Cover and cook gently for about 30 minutes, stirring frequently. Add the sugar and cook for another 5 minutes, or until the onions are softened, reduced and caramelized.

2 Remove the pan from the heat and stir in the flour, then gradually stir in the stock. Return the pan to the heat. Bring to the boil, stirring, then simmer for 3 minutes, or until thickened. Season.

3 Meanwhile, cook the potatoes and the pork and leek sausages. First, cook the potatoes in a pan of boiling salted water for 20 minutes, or until tender.

4 Drain the potatoes well and mash them with the butter, cream and wholegrain mustard. Season with salt and pepper to taste.

5 While the potatoes are cooking, preheat the grill (broiler) to medium. Arrange the sausages in a single layer in the grill pan and cook for 15–20 minutes or until cooked through, turning frequently so that they brown evenly.

6 Serve the sausages with the mashed potatoes and plenty of onion gravy.

INGREDIENTS
serves four

12 pork and leek sausages

salt and ground black pepper

for the onion gravy

30ml | 2 tbsp olive oil

30ml | 2 tbsp butter

8 onions, sliced

5ml | 1 tsp sugar

15ml | 1 tbsp plain (all-purpose) flour

300ml | 1/2 pint | 1 1/4 cups beef stock

for the mashed potatoes

1.4kg | 3 1/4 lb potatoes, peeled and cut into chunks

50g | 2oz | 1/4 cup butter

150ml | 1/4 pint | 2/3 cup double (heavy) cream

15ml/1 tbsp wholegrain mustard

Rich and Filling

On a cold day, there's nothing like the indulgence of a steaming golden sponge pudding, flavoured with maple syrup, or hot poached fruits spiced with cloves and cinnamon. Or enjoy the festive combination of chocolate and orange – a treat that makes winter worth waiting for.

Imagine a hot sponge cake, straight out of the oven but with less golden crust, a deeper sponge and more crumbliness – that's a steamed pudding. It can be flavoured with anything – maple syrup and pecan nuts are wonderful, and look superb when turned out, as here. Serve with lots of your own home-made custard.

STICKY MAPLE and PECAN PUDDING

INGREDIENTS
serves six

60ml | 4 tbsp pure maple syrup

30ml | 2 tbsp fresh brown breadcrumbs

115g | 4oz | 1 cup shelled pecan nuts, roughly chopped

115g | 4oz | 1/2 cup butter, softened

finely grated rind of 1 orange

115g | 4oz | heaped 1/2 cup golden caster (superfine) sugar

2 eggs, beaten

175g | 6oz | 1 1/2 cups self-raising (self-rising) flour, sifted

pinch of salt

about 75ml | 5 tbsp milk

extra maple syrup and home-made custard, to serve

1 Butter a 900ml | 1 1/2 pint | 3 3/4 cup heatproof pudding bowl generously. Stir the maple syrup, breadcrumbs and pecans together and spoon into the bowl.

2 Cream the butter with the orange rind and sugar until light and fluffy. Gradually beat in the eggs, then fold in the flour and salt. Stir in enough milk to make a loose mixture that will drop off the spoon if lightly shaken.

3 Carefully spoon the mixture into the bowl on top of the syrup and nuts. Cover with pleated, buttered baking parchment, then with pleated foil (the pleats allow for expansion). Tie string under the lip of the basin to hold the paper in place, then take it over the top to form a handle.

4 Place the bowl in a pan of simmering water, cover and steam for 2 hours, topping up with boiling water as necessary. Remove the string, foil and paper, then turn out the pudding and serve with extra maple syrup and custard.

COOK'S TIP To make your own pouring custard:
1 Heat 450ml | 3/4 pint | scant 2 cups milk with a few drops of vanilla essence and remove from the heat just as it comes to the boil. Whisk 2 eggs and 1 yolk in a bowl with 30ml | 2 tbsp caster (superfine) sugar. Blend together 15ml | 1 tbsp cornflour (cornstarch) with 30ml | 2 tbsp water and mix with the eggs. Whisk in a little of the hot milk, then add the rest.

2 Strain the egg and milk mixture back into the pan and heat gently, stirring frequently, until the custard thickens sufficiently to coat the back of a wooden spoon.

Fresh apples and pears are combined with dried apricots and figs, and cooked in a fragrant, spicy wine until tender and intensely flavoured.

WINTER FRUIT POACHED in MULLED WINE

INGREDIENTS
serves four

300ml | 1/2 pint | 1¼ cups red wine

300ml | 1/2 pint | 1¼ cups fresh orange juice

finely grated rind and juice of 1 orange

45ml | 3 tbsp clear honey or barley malt syrup

1 cinnamon stick, broken in half

4 cloves

4 cardamom pods, split

2 pears, such as Comice or Williams, peeled, cored and halved

8 ready-to-eat dried figs

12 ready-to-eat dried unsulphured apricots

2 eating apples, peeled, cored and thickly sliced

1 Put the wine, the fresh and squeezed orange juice and half the orange rind in a pan with the honey or syrup and spices. Bring to the boil, then reduce the heat and simmer for 2 minutes, stirring occasionally.

2 Add the pears, figs and apricots to the pan and cook, covered, for 25 minutes, occasionally turning the fruit in the wine mixture. Add the sliced apples and cook for a further 12–15 minutes, until the fruit is tender.

3 Remove the fruit from the pan and discard the spices. Cook the wine mixture over a high heat until reduced and syrupy, then pour it over the fruit. Serve decorated with the reserved strips of orange rind, if wished.

COOK'S TIP Serve with fresh cream, custard, or rice pudding.

This creamy pudding is scented with saffron, cardamom and freshly grated nutmeg. Shelled pistachio nuts give a subtle contrast in colour and add crunch.

INDIAN RICE PUDDING

1 Wash the rice under cold running water and place in a pan with the boiling water. Bring to the boil and boil, uncovered, for 15 minutes.

2 Pour the milk over the rice, then reduce the heat and simmer, partially covered, for 15 minutes.

3 Add the cardamom pods, grated nutmeg, saffron, maize malt syrup and honey, and cook for a further 15 minutes, or until the rice is tender, stirring occasionally.

4 Spoon the rice into small serving bowls and sprinkle with pistachio nuts before serving hot or cold.

COOK'S TIP Rice pudding is delicious served with fresh or dried fruit. Try it with the Winter Fruit Poached in Mulled Wine.

INGREDIENTS
serves four

115g | 4oz | 3/4 cup brown short grain rice

350ml | 12fl oz | 1 1/2 cups boiling water

600ml | 1 pint | 2 1/2 cups milk

6 cardamom pods, bruised

2.5ml | 1/2 tsp freshly grated nutmeg

pinch of saffron threads

60ml | 4 tbsp maize malt syrup

15ml | 1 tbsp clear honey

50g | 2oz | 1/2 cup pistachio nuts, chopped

Everything about this mousse is seductive. The smooth, creamy chocolate lingers on the tongue long after being eaten. Only the best chocolates have this effect, so save your most expensive, cocoa-solids-packed variety for this ultimate indulgence.

CHOCOLATE, ORANGE and LIQUEUR MOUSSE

1 Break the chocolate into pieces and put in a small bowl over a pan of barely simmering water. Pour in the liqueur and add the butter. Leave undisturbed for about 10 minutes, until melted.

2 Separate the eggs and put the whites into a large mixing bowl with a tiny pinch of salt. Stir the chocolate mixture and remove from the heat. Quickly mix in the egg yolks.

3 Whisk the egg whites until stiff but not dry. Fold one large spoonful into the chocolate sauce to loosen the mixture, then carefully, but thoroughly, fold in the remaining egg whites.

4 Spoon the mixture into little pots or ramekins, cover and chill for at least 6 hours, or until set. Serve with thin strips of crystallized orange peel.

INGREDIENTS
serves four

200g | 7oz orange-flavoured dark (bittersweet) chocolate with more than 60% cocoa solids

45ml | 3 tbsp Grand Marnier liqueur

25g/ | 1oz | 2 tbsp unsalted (sweet) butter

3 large (US extra large) eggs

salt

crystallized (candied) orange peel, to serve

This combination of intense flavours produces a very rich dessert, so serve it well chilled and in thin slices. It slices better when it is very cold.

CHOCOLATE CHESTNUT ROULADE

INGREDIENTS
serves ten to twelve

oil, for greasing

175g | 6oz dark chocolate, chopped

30ml | 2 tbsp unsweetened cocoa powder, sifted, plus extra for dusting

50ml | 2fl oz | 1/4 cup freshly brewed strong coffee or espresso

6 eggs, separated

75g | 3oz | 6 tbsp caster (superfine) sugar

pinch of cream of tartar

5ml | 1 tsp vanilla essence (extract)

glacé (candied) chestnuts, to decorate

for the chestnut cream filling

475ml | 16fl oz | 2 cups double (heavy) cream

30ml | 2 tbsp rum or coffee-flavoured liqueur

350g | 12oz can sweetened chestnut purée

115g | 4oz dark chocolate, grated

1 Preheat the oven to 180°C | 350°F | Gas 4. Grease the base and sides of a 39x27x2.5cm | 15½x10½x1in Swiss roll tin (jelly roll pan). Line with baking parchment, allowing a 2.5cm | 1in overhang.

2 Melt the chocolate in the top of a double boiler over a low heat, stirring frequently. Mix the cocoa with the coffee and set aside. In an electric mixer or in a bowl using a whisk, beat the egg yolks with half of the sugar for about 3–5 minutes, until pale and thick. Slowly beat in the melted chocolate and cocoa-coffee paste until just blended.

3 In another bowl, whisk the egg whites and cream of tartar until stiff peaks form. Sprinkle the remaining sugar over in two batches and beat until stiff and glossy, then beat in the vanilla essence. Stir a spoonful of the whisked whites into the chocolate mixture to lighten it, then fold in the remainder. Spoon the mixture into the tin and level the top. Bake for 20–25 minutes, or until the cake springs back when lightly pressed.

4 Meanwhile, dust a clean dishtowel with the extra cocoa powder. As soon as the cake is cooked, carefully turn it out on to the towel and gently peel off the baking parchment from the base. Starting at a narrow end, roll the cake and towel together and cool.

5 To make the filling, whip the cream and rum or liqueur until soft peaks form. Beat a spoonful of cream into the chestnut purée, then fold in the remaining cream and most of the grated chocolate. Unroll the cake and spread 3/4 of the filling to within 2.5cm | 1in of the edges. Gently roll it up, using the towel for support and place seam-side down, on a serving plate. Spoon the reserved chestnut cream into a small icing bag and pipe rosettes along the top. Decorate with glacé chestnuts, grated chocolate and cocoa.

When kumquats are in season, their marvellous spicy-sweet citrus flavour complements both sweet and savoury dishes.

SPICED POACHED KUMQUATS

INGREDIENTS
serves six

450g | 1lb | 4 cups kumquats

115g | 4oz | generous ¹/₂ cup unrefined caster (superfine) sugar or rapadura

150ml | ¹/₄ pint | ²/₃ cup water

1 small cinnamon stick

1 star anise

1 bay leaf, to decorate (optional)

1 Cut the kumquats in half and discard the pips. Place the kumquats in a pan with the sugar, water and spices. Cook over a gentle heat, stirring until the sugar has dissolved.

2 Increase the heat, cover the pan and boil the mixture for 8-10 minutes, until the kumquats are tender. To bottle the kumquats, spoon them into warm, sterilized jars, seal and label. Decorate the kumquats with a bay leaf before serving, if you like.

COOK'S TIP To prepare jars for home preserves, preheat the oven to 160°C | 325°F | Gas 3. Wash the jars in hot soapy water, rinse and dry thoroughly. Place the jars in the oven for 10 minutes, then turn off the oven and leave to cool.

The combination of light Italian fruit bread, apricots and pecan nuts produces a wonderfully rich version of traditional bread-and-butter pudding.

APRICOT PANETTONE PUDDING

1 Grease a 1 litre | 1³/₄ pint | 4 cup baking dish. Arrange half the panettone in the base of the dish, scatter over half the pecan nuts and all the dried apricots, then add another layer of panettone on top, spreading it as evenly as you can.

2 Pour the milk into a small pan and add the vanilla essence. Warm the milk over a medium heat until it just simmers. In a large bowl, mix together the beaten egg and maple syrup, grate in the nutmeg, then whisk in the hot milk.

3 Preheat the oven to 200°C | 400°F | Gas 6. Pour the milk mixture over the panettone, lightly pressing down each slice so that it is totally submerged in the mixture. Set the dish aside and leave the pudding to stand for at least 10 minutes.

4 Scatter the reserved pecan nuts over the top and sprinkle with the demerara sugar and nutmeg. Bake for about 40 minutes, until risen and golden.

COOK'S TIP Panettone is a sweet Italian yeast bread made with raisins, citron, pine nuts and star anise. If it is not available, use any sweet yeasted fruit loaf instead.

INGREDIENTS
serves six

unsalted (sweet) butter, for greasing

350g | 12oz panettone, sliced into triangles

25g | 1oz | ¼ cup pecan nuts

75g | 3oz | ⅓ cup ready-to-eat dried apricots, chopped

500ml | 17fl oz | 2¼ cups semi-skimmed (low-fat) milk

5ml | 1 tsp vanilla essence

1 large (US extra large) egg, beaten

30ml | 2 tbsp maple syrup

2.5ml | ½ tsp grated nutmeg, plus extra for sprinkling

demerara (raw) sugar, for sprinkling

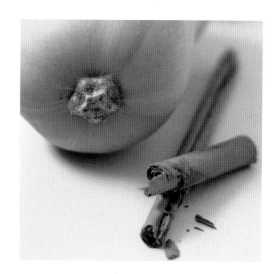

The bright orange colour and warming flavour of this marmalade is guaranteed to banish the winter blues.

PUMPKIN and ORANGE MARMALADE

1 Squeeze the juice from the oranges, remove the membranes and reserve with the pips (seeds). Thinly slice the peel and place in a large pan with the sliced lemons. Tie the pips and membranes in a muslin (cheesecloth) bag with the spices. Add to the citrus fruit with the water. Bring to the boil, then cover and simmer for 1 hour, or until the fruit is tender.

2 Add the pumpkin and continue cooking for 1½ hours, or until very tender. Remove the muslin bag, squeeze out over the pan and then discard.

3 Stir in the sugar over a low heat until completely dissolved. Increase the heat and boil for a further 10–15 minutes, or until the marmalade becomes quite thick and reaches setting point.

4 Remove the pan from the heat and skim off any scum from the surface using a slotted spoon. Leave to cool for 5 minutes then pour into warm sterilized jars. Seal and label, then store in a cool, dark place.

COOK'S TIP To test for the setting point, spoon a small quantity on to a chilled saucer, chill for 3 minutes, then push the mixture with your finger. If wrinkles form on the surface, it is ready. Alternatively, you could use a sugar thermometer clipped to the side of the pan, but not touching the base. When the temperature reaches 105°C|220°F, the marmalade is ready.

INGREDIENTS
makes 2.75kg|6lb

900g | 2lb Seville (Temple) oranges, washed and halved

450g | 1lb lemons, halved and thinly sliced

2 cinnamon sticks

2.5cm | 1in piece fresh root ginger, peeled and thinly sliced

1.5ml | ¼ tsp grated nutmeg

1.75 litres | 3 pints | 7½ cups water

800g | 1¾lb pumpkin, peeled, seeds removed, and thinly sliced

1.3kg | 3lb | 6¾ cups warmed sugar

INDEX

NOTES

For all recipes, quantities are given in both metric and imperial measures and, where appropriate, measures are also given in standard cups and spoons. Follow one set, but not a mixture, because they are not interchangeable.

Standard spoon and cup measures are level.
1 tsp = 5ml, 1 tbsp = 15ml, 1 cup = 250ml | 8fl oz

Medium eggs are used unless otherwise stated.

This edition published in the UK in 2008 by
Apple Press
7 Greenland Street
London NW1 0ND
www.apple-press.com

ISBN: 978 1 84543 265 2

This book was designed and produced by
Anness Publishing Ltd
Hermes House
88–89 Blackfriars Road
London SE1 8HA
www.annesspublishing.com